# Inheritance
# in Ontario

# Inheritance in Ontario

## Wills and Other Records for Family Historians

JANE E. MACNAMARA

DUNDURN
TORONTO

Editor: Allison Hirst
Design: Jesse Hooper
Printer: Webcom

**Library and Archives Canada Cataloguing in Publication**

MacNamara, Jane E. (Jane Ellen), 1956-
    Inheritance in Ontario : wills and other records for family historians / by Jane E. MacNamara.

(Genealogist's reference shelf)
Co-published by Ontario Genealogical Society.
Includes bibliographical references and index.
Issued also in electronic format.
ISBN 978-1-4597-0580-7

    1. Inheritance and succession--Ontario--History--Sources. 2. Probate records--Ontario--Sources. 3. Ontario--Genealogy--Handbooks, manuals, etc. I. Ontario Genealogical Society II. Title. III. Series: Genealogist's reference shelf

CS88.O6M23 2013        929.3713        C2012-907674-0

1  2  3  4  5     17  16  15  14  13

Conseil des Arts du Canada    Canada Council for the Arts    Canada    ONTARIO ARTS COUNCIL / CONSEIL DES ARTS DE L'ONTARIO

We acknowledge the support of the **Canada Council for the Arts** and the **Ontario Arts Council** for our publishing program. We also acknowledge the financial support of the **Government of Canada** through the **Canada Book Fund** and **Livres Canada Books**, and the **Government of Ontario** through the **Ontario Book Publishing Tax Credit** and the **Ontario Media Development Corporation**.

Care has been taken to trace the ownership of copyright material used in this book. The author and the publisher welcome any information enabling them to rectify any references or credits in subsequent editions.

*J. Kirk Howard, President*

Printed and bound in Canada.

**VISIT US AT**
*Dundurn.com* | *Definingcanada.ca* | *@dundurnpress* | *Facebook.com/dundurnpress*

Ontario Genealogical Society
Suite 102, 40 Orchard View Boulevard
Toronto, Ontario, Canada M4R 1B9
tel. (416) 489-0734    fax. (416) 489-9803
*provoffice@ogs.on.ca    www.ogs.on.ca*

| Dundurn | Gazelle Book Services Limited | Dundurn |
|---|---|---|
| 3 Church Street, Suite 500 | White Cross Mills | 2250 Military Road |
| Toronto, Ontario, Canada | High Town, Lancaster, England | Tonawanda, NY |
| M5E 1M2 | L41 4XS | U.S.A. 14150 |

*In appreciation of my great, great aunt Catherine
who died in 1889 without writing a will.
Her estate file provided the names, locations, and
signatures of all her siblings —
and is one of the best records of my MacNamara family.*

# CONTENTS

# PREFACE AND ACKNOWLEDGEMENTS

As a family historian, I've found some wonderful estate files. I appreciate the family connections the documents proved and the insight into the life and times, and sometimes characters, of the people involved. I'm also a fan of understanding the process — seeing each piece of the estate file build to a conclusion and link to related records.

I had a lot of help from folks at libraries and archives while researching this book.

First and foremost, I would like to thank the staff at the Archives of Ontario — the reading room staff, those who fetched and carried and re-filed original records for me and those who answered, or tried valiantly to answer, my really difficult questions with a smile and genuine curiosity. I appreciated Paul McIlroy's and Charles Levi's insight into surrogate court records.

I am enormously grateful to the creators of and contributors to the Archives Descriptive Database and all the other painstakingly compiled finding aids at the archives. What would we ever do without you?

Thanks to Glenn Wright for digging into the background of some Library and Archives Canada records for me and to Yvonne Sorenson from the Family History Library in Salt Lake City for her work on the same records.

I would also like to acknowledge the efforts of Gloria Hunter, Wayne County Register of Deeds, Detroit; Dawn Eurich, archivist, Special Collections, Detroit Public Library; Tom Belton, senior archivist, Western University Archives and Research Collections Centre; Krista Richardson, Prince Edward County Archives; and Alexandra McEwen, Library and Archives Canada.

Some very clever folks read the manuscript, or parts of it, for me: Kathy Baker, Ruth Burkholder, Ruth Chernia, Brenda Dougall Merriman, and Kathie Orr. Lee Dickson, Ron Junkin, and Janice Nickerson provided suggestions and help along the way.

And a special thanks to all the students in my Hands-on Ontario Estate Records courses, for helping me to understand the records and sharing my fascination for both the search and the story revealed.

# INTRODUCTION

While it is true that not everyone left a will or had a court-appointed administrator look after their affairs, many people who lived in Ontario did. Certainly no genealogical search is complete without a thorough search for an estate file.

Estate files can help you prove a death — a person had to be dead before their estate was distributed, or at least their relatives and the courts had to be convinced that they were no longer living.

In the absence of a death registration or record of burial, an estate file can provide an exact or at least an approximate death date to narrow your search. Family (or others) could not apply to the courts to administer the estate until at least a week after the death (two weeks if no will was written).[1] If there is a will in the estate file, the time between its signing and the application to administer the estate provides a finite window in which the death must have occurred. In many cases it is a narrow window — a matter of a few months.

There may be clues as to the testator's state of health in the will itself, as blatant as phrases like "being weak in body" or as subtle as a reference to a child "not yet born" or a shaky signature.

1. *General Rules and Orders of the Surrogate Courts, Upper Canada* (Toronto: Thompson and Company, 1858), 2.

Clues to the testator's religious affiliation, educational background, and community involvement may be revealed in his or her bequests to charities.

An estate file rarely specifies the age of the testator, but references to family members and the possessions the person has accumulated may indicate whether advanced age compelled the testator to write a will or whether some other circumstance has inspired a younger person to acknowledge his or her mortality. A soldier might write his will before going into battle. A traveller might put his or her affairs in order before embarking on a significant voyage. Recent events — a marriage, birth of a child or grandchild, death of a spouse or parent, the acquisition of property, the launch of a new business or partnership — may also be triggers for the writing of a will.

Estate files may also provide family connections and indicate whether a particular relative survived to inherit or to act as administrator. If the person was married, the spouse is almost always mentioned in a will, although not always by name. Children were often mentioned, but again, not necessarily by name and some of the children might not be mentioned at all. However, there is an excellent chance that an estate file may provide names and locations of adult children and married names of daughters.

Is your ancestor's name missing from his parent's will? It was quite common for a parent to omit the name of one or more of his or her offspring (particularly adult sons or daughters) as beneficiaries. This doesn't necessarily mean that the parent and child are estranged, or that the child has died. The parent may have provided a generous dowry for a daughter or set a son up in business. Consider those possibilities before you conclude that there was a rift.

And there could be a surprise. Offspring from previous marriages (or other alliances) may be acknowledged in a will.

Names of siblings and more distant relations of the deceased may also be found in an estate file in several different contexts.

They may be beneficiaries of the estate, in which case the testator usually states the relationship — "John Smith, son of my late brother Fred." They may be involved in the administration of the estate, or step aside to allow another person to administer — in either case they will be well documented. Other relations, particularly earlier generations, may be mentioned as previous owners of property being bequeathed — "the silver spoons left to me by my great aunt Matilda Smith."

Some of the most fruitful estate records in my own research have been from family members outside my direct line. I treasure those childless aunts and uncles whose estates were left to meticulously named nieces and nephews and their descendants. Be sure to broaden your search for estate files beyond your direct ancestors.

Because the authenticity of the will, inventory, supporting documents, and the qualification of the administrator(s) had to be proven before a judge, estate files are considered to be very reliable evidence. However, be cautious that the individual documents may be copies of originals, so transcription errors may be present. Consider whether the information in the document was given by a first-hand informant. Did the testator, or the informant, or the clerk all know how to spell that surname or place name? Maybe not.

We're very lucky in Ontario to have access to a broad range of records of inheritance for most eras. We can look at the documents collected and created to apply for letters of administration or letters probate in an estate file. We can often also follow the case through court minutes and registers to find the complete story. Each of these records may add an important tidbit — perhaps a relationship or a place of residence — that can add to your family history. Many of these records are also available on interloan from the Archives of Ontario and worldwide through FamilySearch.org.

## WHERE IN ONTARIO DID MY ANCESTOR LIVE?

Understanding the geography, political divisions, and legal jurisdictions of where and when your ancestors lived is a really important tool in family history research. The following pages provide just enough guidance to help you find and identify records of inheritance. I encourage you to learn all you can about the location and times of your ancestors to help with this and other research. You'll find a list of basic sources at the end of this chapter.

Most government agencies organize their records geographically and the courts that handled estate matters in Ontario are no exception.

First, some words about the place we call "Ontario":

- Until 1791, it was part of Quebec.
- In 1791, the western part of Quebec became Upper Canada.
- In 1841, Upper Canada became Canada West.
- In 1867, Canada West became Ontario.

The political divisions within Ontario were adjusted and became more complex as the European population grew. For example, the four enormous Districts set out in 1788 — in a rather arbitrary way — were divided into twenty more practical Districts by 1849.

### Districts

If you are looking for a record of inheritance between 1787 and 1793, it is important to find out in which of the four original Districts your ancestor lived to know the correct prerogative court. The Districts were Luneburg, Mecklenburg, Nassau, and Hesse — changed in 1792 to Eastern, Midland, Home, and Western, respectively.

Starting in the east, Luneburg District covered the area from the present Quebec border to a line running north from the mouth of the Gananoque River. Mecklenburg District spanned from the Gananoque River to a line running north from the mouth of the Trent River. Nassau District ran from the Trent River to a line running north from Long Point. Hesse District covered the part of the province west of Long Point — including a large portion of what is now the state of Michigan.

The original four Districts were divided many times into twenty smaller jurisdictions. From 1793 to 1849, each District had its own surrogate court. Estate files for this period are centrally indexed, making it unnecessary to search by District.

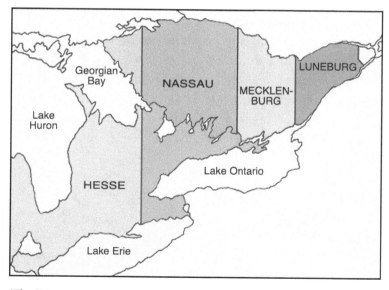

*The Districts set out in 1788 were Luneburg, Mecklenburg, Nassau, and Hesse — changed in 1792 to Eastern, Midland, Home, and Western, respectively. (Map by Jane E. MacNamara)*

## Counties

In 1849, the Districts were abolished and local government switched to the county level. (Counties had existed since 1792, but only as a division for land registry, militia, and electoral purposes.) Surrogate courts were established in each county, or sometimes in a group of two or more "united counties." The united counties may have separated or regrouped through the years, so it is important to know the status of the county during the period you are searching. Knowing in which county your ancestor lived and died can significantly accelerate the search. But if you don't know, there are ways to get around the problem. Read on.

## Townships, Towns, and Cities

While estate records are not arranged by this level of municipality, the testator will usually be identified by his or her former residence — a rural township, a town, or a city. It is a good way to recognize which estate record belongs to your ancestor. Land records, another important source for information about inheritance, are arranged by township, town, or city. Knowing the exact location is crucial for their use.

## SUGGESTED FURTHER READING

Armstrong, Frederick H. *Handbook of Upper Canadian Chronology.* Toronto: Dundurn Press, 1985.

Dunford, Fraser. *Municipal Records in Ontario.* Toronto: Ontario Genealogical Society, 2005.

Mika, Nick, and Helma Mika. *Places in Ontario: Their Name Origins and History.* 3 volumes. Belleville, ON: Mika Publishing, 1977.

# CHAPTER I

## *Where to Look and What You Might Find*

For the most part, estate records were created by courts. This chapter will help you decide which court's records might contain your ancestor's will or administration and the documents that were created around it. I'll explain some of the terminology you'll see in estate records and show you some examples of estate records from various courts — and what they can add to your ancestor's story.

### WHICH COURT DO I LOOK AT?

Use this table as a guide to the records to search for each time period. Be aware that many wills and administrations were processed a considerable time — sometimes years — after the death.

Before 1788    Look at Quebec notarial records, which included notaries resident in the Detroit area. From 1777, records might be found in the Montreal District Prerogative Court. See chapter 2.

1788–1792    Look at the District Prerogative Courts. Notarial records also continued into this era. See chapter 2.

1793–1858    If your ancestor owned land in more than one District, look at the Court of Probate. See chapter 3.
              If your ancestor owned land in one District, look at the District surrogate court, then the Court of Probate. See chapters 3 and 4.

1859–today    Look at the records of the county surrogate court. See chapter 4.


## WHERE ARE THE RECORDS KEPT?

You may find small collections of microfilmed copies of records of local interest at libraries and archives around the province, but the main sources for original and filmed records are the following repositories:

- **Archives of Ontario**
  134 Ian Macdonald Boulevard
  Toronto, Ontario M7A 2C5
  *www.archives.gov.on.ca*
  The Archives of Ontario is the main repository for court records for Ontario. Many are also available through interloan.

- **FamilySearch.org**
  35 North West Temple Street
  Salt Lake City, Utah 84150
  *. familysearch.org*
  FamilySearch.org is a non-profit family history organization with the largest genealogical library in

the world (in Salt Lake City) and a network of some 4,500 Family History Centres around the world. FamilySearch.org is also an important online source of information and a rapidly growing collection of digitized records. Many Ontario court records are available on microfilm from the organization.

- **Library and Archives Canada** (see chapters 2 and 4)
  395 Wellington Street
  Ottawa, Ontario K1A 0N4
  *www.bac-lac.gc.ca*
  Our national archives holds some early records of inheritance.

- **Prince Edward County Archives**
  261 Main Street
  Wellington, Ontario K0K 3L0
  By special agreement with the Archives of Ontario, the Prince Edward County Archives holds an extensive collection of original local estate files. See chapter 4 for details.

- **Detroit Public Library, Burton Historical Collection**
  5201 Woodward Avenue
  Detroit, Michigan 48202
  *www.detroit.lib.mi.us*
  The Burton Historical Collection holds early records for the Detroit/Windsor area. See chapter 2.

- **Wayne County Register of Deeds**
400 Monroe
7th Floor
Detroit, Michigan 48226-2925
*www.co.wayne.mi.us/deeds.htm*
This very busy government office holds some
early records for the Detroit/Windsor area. See
chapter 2.

## WHAT'S IN A WILL?

In the course of my research for this book, I've looked at a lot
of dry lists of rules and regulations for writing wills and taking
them through the court process. My favourite book, by far, is a
little manual for Upper Canadians written in 1841 by W.C. Keele.
*A Brief View of the Laws of Upper Canada Up to the Present Time*,
published in Toronto by W.J. Coates, is preserved in the library
of the Archives of Ontario. It covers everything you'd want to
know, from assessments to how to collect the bounty on wolves.
(If the treasurer was short of cash, the bounty could offset your
taxes owed.)

On pages 92 to 100, Keele explains "Executors and Wills."
Although the laws have been adjusted many times during the
intervening time, Keele's picture of the situation in 1841 is of
interest.

- A will capable of passing real property had to be
in writing with at least two witnesses.
- A will for personal property could be written by
the testator or by his directions, with no witnesses.
- If the testator was on his deathbed he could
speak his wishes in the presence of witnesses.

This was a nuncupative will. There were restrictions: the value of the estate had to be of £30 or less unless proved by the oaths of three witnesses; the testator had to be in his own home or where he had lived for ten days, unless he was taken sick away from home; he had to die within six months of speaking the will; and a nuncupative will had to be written down within six days.

- A married woman couldn't make a will unless her husband was banished for life by an act of parliament.
- "Infants" could make a will of personal property — males at age fourteen, females at twelve.
- If a man died intestate, real estate went to his eldest son (after payment of debts and the wife's dower third). If the eldest son had died it went to the next son, but if no sons, the property would be divided equally amongst his daughters.
- If the man had no children, real estate went to his father, then eldest brother, then younger brothers. If none were living then it went to the deceased's grandfather, then uncles. Only after all these choices would it revert back to the wife's relatives.
- If all else fails, the property goes to the Crown.
- Personal property of an intestate person was divided differently: one-third to the wife, the rest divided equally among all the children. If there were no children, one moiety went to the wife and the rest was divided among other members of the family.

# SOME BASIC TERMS FOUND IN ONTARIO ESTATE RECORDS

**Administrator/administratrix:** The person, or one of the persons appointed by the court to look after the distribution of the estate.

**Codicil:** A deposition made before witnesses that changes one or more of the provisions of a will. A codicil often reflects a change in the financial position of the testator or the death of an heir named in the will.

**Executor/executrix:** The person, or one of the persons named in a will to look after distributing the estate. The executor/executrix is not obligated by law to act as administrator.

**Intestate:** Describes a person who has died without making a will.

**Letters of administration with will annexed:** In this type of administration, the testator has expressed his or her wishes about how the estate is to be distributed, either in a will that is not valid or in a letter or similar document, or all the executors have since died.

**Testate:** Describes a person who has died after making a will.

**Will:** A deposition made before witnesses that outlines the deceased's final wishes.

# A TASTE OF ONTARIO ESTATE RECORDS

## 1. Elijah Peet

Elijah Peet's estate file is in the Surrogate Court of the District of Johnstown in Upper Canada (Leeds and Grenville United Counties Surrogate Court estate files, RG 22-179, MS 638, reel 28, Archives of Ontario).

Elijah died in 1803. I know this because letters of administration were issued on 5 January 1804. By law, since Elijah had not written a valid will, the administrators had to wait at least two weeks to apply to the court.

An estate file is a collection of documents that were either presented to the court or issued by the court, relating to the distribution of an individual's worldly goods — whether or not the person had a will.

In Elijah's file, I found the following documents:

- Administration bond of £100 from administrator Peet Selee, with Samuel and Levius Sherwood, issued 5 January 1804
- A "true and perfect inventory"
- Wording for an ad for the "vendue" of Elijah's possessions
- An accounting of the vendue (who bought what items)
- An account of expenses incurred by the administrator

What can we glean from each of these documents?

Let's begin with the bond. Although we don't have his application, the fact that Peet Selee was appointed administrator means that the court felt he was a suitable choice. He may have been a relative, or it could be that the relatives stepped aside and did not challenge his appointment. Peet could write, and fairly confidently. Peet Selee [Seelye] is called "yeoman" of Elizabethtown. The other names on the bond, Samuel and Levius Sherwood, were both prominent citizens and court officials. They were probably chosen because they were good for the £100 rather than for a relationship with the deceased.

Next is the inventory. It was one of the responsibilities of administrator Peet Selee, and the belongings of Elijah Peet were appraised on 28 March by David Alexander and Isaac Booth and the inventory filed with the court on 29 March 1804. It included:

> 1 mare and colt
> 1 bridle
> 1 pair saddle bags
> 1 great coat, pair of boots, pair of shoes
> 1 shaving box, 1 razor and case
> Set of shoemaker's tools, bag and leather apron
> 3 lasts, 2 coats, 2 vests, 2 pr of pantaloons
> 1 pair of trousers, 3 shirts, 4 pairs of stockings
> 4 muslin handkerchiefs, 1 silk handkerchief
> 1 cotton handkerchief, 1 snuff box, 1 knife
> 1 pocket book, 1 pinchbeck watch
> 1 pair of galoshes, 1 hat and cover

The belongings added up to £25, 18 shillings. I find it curious that Elijah seems to have had no household goods — not a stick of furniture or a cooking utensil. It looks like he could pack just about everything into his saddlebags. Was he an itinerant shoemaker or an elderly boarder, perhaps?

The next document is an advertisement for a "vendue" of the property of Elijah Peet, deceased. The vendue (a period word for a public sale) was to be held on 7 April 1804, at the inn of James Curtis in Elizabethtown.

The vendue, under the auspices of Vendue Master Jonathan Mills Church, seems to have been moderately successful. Everything was sold and the amount earned was less than £1 under the appraised amount. The list of buyers, though, is short: William Jones, Justice Seely, Reuben Mott, Elias Peck, Phillip Masterson, and Jehisda Boice. Jonathan Mills Church himself bought two pair of stockings, and Peet Selee acquired eleven items, including the mare and colt and the pinchbeck watch. (Elias Peck became the proud owner of the galoshes for six shillings.)

The final document is an account of the expenses incurred by Peet Selee on behalf of the estate, and perhaps also during Elijah's last months. It is difficult to read, but it seems to go back to October 1802, when Elijah owed Peet Selee for a quantity of pork and three quarts of salt, a three point blanket, a large powder horn, shoeing a horse, and "working and mending." Selee seems also to have made traps and carried them to the river for Elijah.

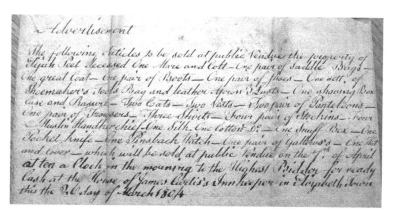

*Ad for a vendue of the belongings of Elijah Peet who died in Johnstown District in 1803. (Archives of Ontario RG 22-179 Leeds and Grenville United Counties Surrogate Court estate files, film MS 638-28, arranged alphabetically)*

The next expense is 15 shillings for "The Search of him Before he was found," followed by charges for letters of administration, keeping Elijah's horses, setting up the vendue, and other incidentals up to at least the day of the auction. The expenses total £25 and 17 shillings — unfortunately a shilling less than the inventory evaluation, but a little more than what was raised by the auction.

## 2. John Stacy

John Stacy's estate file is recorded on the first pages of London District Surrogate Court Register Book A at the Archives of Ontario (RG 22-320, barcode D757015, box D408591). The first document in the register is Stacy's will, transcribed in full here:

> In the Name of God Amen
>
> I John Stacy of the township of Charlotteville in the County of Norfolk and Western District of the Province of Upper Canada being in good health of body and of sound and perfect mind and memory thanks be to almighty God for his unbounded mercy and goodness towards the children of men and calling to mind the uncertainty of this present life and that it is ordained for all Flesh once to die, do make and publish this as and for my last Will and Testament in manner and form following, that is to say
>
> First, I give and bequeath my immortal soul unto Almighty God who gave it being, and my body to the Dust from whence it came, in sure and perfect hope and belief of a joyous resurrection.

*Register copy of the 1799 will of John Stacy, proved in 1800. (Archives of Ontario RG 22-320 Middlesex County Surrogate Court registers, London District Surrogate Court Register Book A, 1800–1817, page 1)*

Item. I give, devise and bequeath unto my loving daughter Elizabeth Stacy, and to my loving stepson Moses Rice and to their and each of their heirs, executors, administrators and assigns forever all the lands and tenements, goods and chattels, generally all the whole estate both real and personal, that I shall or may be legally possessed of at the time of my decease, after the decease of my loving wife Maiden Stacy and myself, and after all my just debts and funeral charges shall have been well and truly paid and satisfied by my executors hereinafter named to be equally divided between them, the said Elizabeth Stacy and Moses Rice, share and share alike, regard being had to quantity, quality and valuation.

Item. It is hereby and herein to be particularly observed, that if at any time hereafter during my natural life the above named Moses Rice shall cease to continue in my family and perform the duty of an adopted son, that then, and in that case this my last will and testament so far as it relates to and concerns him the said Moses Rice, shall be null and void to all intents and purposes as if the same had never been made: anything herein before contained, mentioned or expressed to the contrary in anywise notwithstanding. And I do hereby authorize, nominate, constitute and appoint my trusty and well beloved friends William Cope of the Township of Walsingham, and Robert Monro of the Township of Charlotteville, to be executors of this my last Will and Testament. In

Witness whereof I have hereunto set my hand and affixed my seal this twenty second day of August in the year of our Lord 1799.

Signed: John Stacy

Signed, sealed, published and declared by the above named John Stacy, to be his last Will and Testament in the presence of us, who have hereunto subscribed our names as witnesses in the presence of the Testator.

Signed:
Joseph Colver
William Culver
Joseph Miller

Document two in the register is an oath by two of the witnesses to Stacy's signature: "The above will was duly proved by the oath of the above named William Culver and Joseph Miller the eighteenth day of October in the year of our Lord 1800. [Signed] Thomas Welch, Reg Sur Court."

Document three is a citation issued on 25 October 1800 to executors William Cope and Robert Monro. They appeared and declined to act as administrators.

Document four is the petition of Maiden Stacy, John Stacy's widow, who applied to administer the estate on 25 October 1800. The document states that John Stacy died on 18 November 1799. The fact that William Cope and Robert Monro have declined is acknowledged.

Document five is the grant of letters of administration. This document, also dated 25 October, restates that Cope and Monro have declined the executorship, and states that Thomas Smith and his wife Elizabeth, the daughter of John Stacy, have also declined to administer, leaving Maiden Stacy as the "nearest of kin." Administration is granted to Maiden Stacy. She had to give a bond and security.

Document six is a warrant of appraisement, also dated 25 October. It appoints Peter Teeple and William Culver to appraise the inventory that Maiden Stacy shows them.

In document seven, dated 15 June 1800, Maiden Stacy swears to "truly and justly administer," pay all legacies and debts, and make an inventory of all the "goods, chattels, rights, credits and effects" of her late husband. She will show the inventory to the appraisers, and then take the inventory and certified appraisal back to the court "with all convenient speed."

Document eight is the inventory. This listing, dated 16 June 1800, includes lands and tenements worth £156, an account against John Backhouse for £6, and the following items:

> 4 cows and three heifers
> 2 yoke of steers and 1 bull
> 3 calves
> 1 yoke of oxen
> 6 sheep
> 3 hogs
> 1 pair of stilyards [probably a pair of steelyards, a counter-balance scale]
> 2 plowshears & a harrow
> 2 iron pots
> 1 frying pan
> 1 dresser
> 16 earthen plates
> 2 pewter basons & 1 platter
> 1 tea pot
> 1 gun

2 oxes

1 chest and bread box

2 hoes

1 chest

1 loom & tackling

1 churn & pail

2 chains

a horse

The total value of the estate was appraised at £260. The appraisers swore to have been honest and impartial on 17 June 1800.

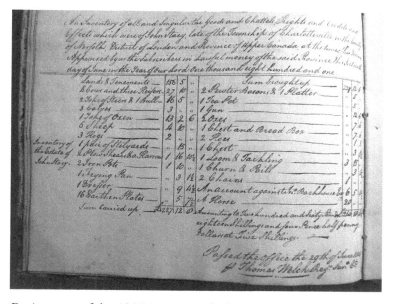

*Register copy of the 1800 inventory of John Stacy. (Archives of Ontario RG 22-320 Middlesex County Surrogate Court registers, London District Surrogate Court Register Book A, 1800–1817, page 4)*

## 3. Catherine MacNamara

Catherine MacNamara's estate file is in the records of the Surrogate Court of the County of York (Grant number 13075, February 20, 1899, RG 22-179, GS 1-1070, Archives of Ontario). This estate file shows the additional documentation required after the 1858 reorganization of the surrogate courts. Although there was no will, the file is very informative about family connections. The file contains the following documents:

- Order that letters of administration be issued to John and Patrick MacNamara. Includes a memorandum of the fees paid.
- Cover page with a checklist of the various papers "hereunto annexed" that were submitted to the court.
- Certification from the Surrogate Clerk that he has received no other application to administer the estate.
- Certification from the Surrogate Clerk that he has searched for and not found a copy of a will filed with his office for safekeeping.
- Petition from John and Patrick MacNamara to administer. The document gives Catherine's death date and lists her siblings (John, Patrick, Ellen Canney, Cornelius, and Timothy) as next of kin.
- Affidavit from John stating that he doesn't know the whereabouts of brother Timothy.
- Document from Cornelius renouncing administration in favour of "my eldest brother John MacNamara and my brother Patrick."

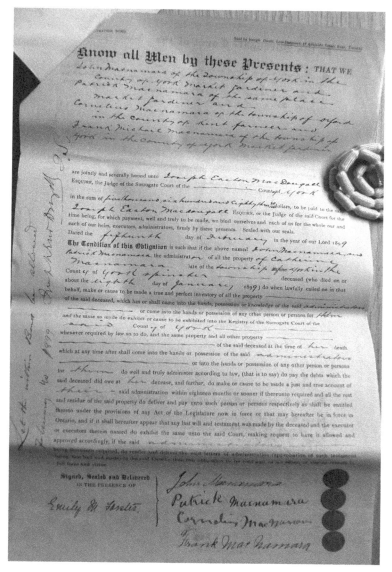

*Administration bond from the estate file of Catherine MacNamara, 1899, with signatures of her three brothers and nephew Frank. (Archives of Ontario RG 22-179 County of York Surrogate Court, Grant number 13075, film GS 1-1070)*

- Document from Ellen Canney renouncing administration in favour of "my eldest brother John MacNamara and my brother Patrick."
- Affidavit from Patrick that he has searched for will and believes Catherine died intestate.
- Affidavit from Patrick that Catherine died 8 January 1899, in the Township of York.
- Inventory of Catherine's estate, consisting of only a debenture from the Canada Permanent Loan Company worth $1,600 and $1,241.90 cash in the bank.
- Oath from Patrick that Catherine's personal estate was worth less than $3,000 and that she owned no real estate.
- Oaths from Patrick and John that they will "faithfully administer" the property.
- Administration bond for $5,683 from John and Patrick, their brother Cornelius, and John's son Frank MacNamara. It includes the signatures of all four men.
- Affidavit from Cornelius and Frank that they are sureties on the administration bond.

Catherine's estate file does not confirm how the money was disbursed. This is not unusual. With most estate files we are left to assume that administrators followed the will's directives, or if there was no will, the estate was divided fairly in compliance with the law. The court made the same assumption unless someone complained. In Catherine MacNamara's case, her administrators swore to distribute the estate according to law. Her siblings, John, Patrick, Cornelius, and Ellen, would have inherited equally. There is no indication that a portion was reserved for the missing brother, Timothy.

# CHAPTER 2

## Early Records of Inheritance, 1763 to 1793 or Thereabouts

From the 1763 Treaty of Paris until 1791, the huge area we know as Ontario was all part of Quebec. Before the influx of Loyalists in 1783, there were really very few Europeans settled permanently in "Western" Quebec. The exception was the Windsor/Detroit area, where in 1701 a French settlement was founded at Detroit and other small settlements had grown over the next sixty years. There was also an agricultural settlement at Niagara to support the garrison there.

### NOTARIAL RECORDS

The earliest records of inheritance — and just about every other legal or official matter — were created by notaries, justices of the peace, or record keepers. (The duties were similar or overlapping and the positions were often held by the same man.) Their knowledge of the law, or at least of the bureaucracy, made them powerful. The most prominent among them in the Detroit/Windsor area seem to have been:

- 1730–circa 1765       Robert Navarre
- circa 1765–circa 1778    Philippe Dejean
- 1779–1784           Thomas Williams
- 1784–1792           Guillaume Monforton

Unfortunately, their records are somewhat elusive. I found records in three locations: the Wayne County Register of Deeds in Detroit, the Detroit Public Library's Burton Historical Collection, and Library and Archives Canada. (See chapter 1 for contact information.)

**The Wayne County Register of Deeds** holds three original registers:

- Register A covers the period from April 1766 to February 1776. Notary Philippe Dejean's name appears on nearly all records.
- Register B covers the period from January 1776 to May 1780. The notary is Philippe Dejean, with notary Thomas Williams appearing in May 1779.
- Register C covers the period from May 1780 to 1795, with few records beyond 1785. The name of notary Thomas Williams can be found on most records, with the addition of Guillaume Monforton on later records.

These large volumes were re-bound at some point.[2] The now sepia-coloured ink is still quite readable, although many of the earliest pages have been coated with a shellac to preserve them. (The shellac has yellowed, of course.) The records in the registers are mostly in French and include land transfers, marriage

2. Registers A, B, and C were moved to Detroit from Windsor in 1871 according to a note in the John Askin Papers, Quaife, Milo M., *The John Askin Papers, Volume 1: 1747–1795* (Detroit: Detroit Public Library, 1928), 107.

contracts, and other financial records. The most apparent records of inheritance are inventories of the possessions of a deceased person. For example, in Register A, the inventory of Madame Chabert, dated 13 May 1773, fills four and a half pages and details her belongings room by room. Every silver *fourchette et cuillère*, furniture, linens, and clothing are listed, providing a wonderful glimpse of what seems to have been a comfortable household.

**The Detroit Public Library's Burton Historical Collection** has a series of volumes known as "Detroit Notarial Records."

- Volume A 1763–1776 is a handwritten transcription of Register A at the Wayne County Register of Deeds as described previously. Note that the start date varies from what I observed at the Register of Deeds.

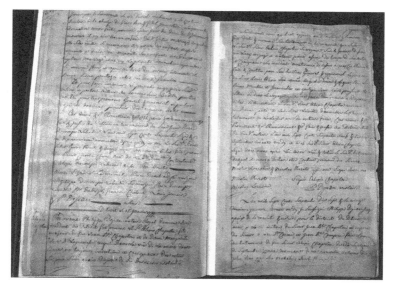

*Record of the opening of the will of Alexis Chapoton in 1777 and acceptance as valid by notary Philippe Dejean, in Register B at the Wayne County Register of Deeds, Detroit.*

- Volume B 1776–1780 is a handwritten transcription of Register B at the Wayne County Register of Deeds as described previously.
- Volume C 1780–1795 is a handwritten transcription of Register C at the Wayne County Register of Deeds as described previously.
- Index 1737 to 1795 is a typed index to the principal names mentioned in volumes A, B, and C. The type of record — inventory, land transfer, marriage contract, etc. — is not identified.
- Volume D, Part 1, is a negative photostat of the first half of the original register of notary Guillaume Monforton. The first few pages of this volume tell the story of how the records were preserved and made their way to Detroit. The pages include an 1860 affidavit by notary Guillaume Monforton's grandson (another Guillaume Monforton) stating that the book had been in his father's and then his possession until 1858 when he gave it to Charles Labadie of Windsor. A second 1860 affidavit, by Labadie, says that he delivered the book to John Stuart of the Town of Windsor in 1859. This may have been a loan or a place to keep the register safe, because other sources say Labadie left it to the Dominion Archives in Ottawa. Certainly, it is at the successor institution, Library and Archives Canada, today. In 1926 the Wayne County Register of Deeds requested it be returned through the British ambassador. Because it covered Canadian as well as American territory, it was apparently not returned, and Detroit had to make do with a photostatic copy. An international incident seems to have been avoided! See

also "Records of Pioneers Retained in Canada" in the Toronto *Globe*, 25 August 1926, page 3.

- Volume D, Part 2, is a negative photostat of the second half of the original register of notary Guillaume Monforton.
- Volume D 1786–1793 is a handwritten copy of the Monforton register.

*Record of a 1788 protest lodged before notary Guillaume Monforton by James McDonnell on behalf of Niagara merchants Hamilton and Cartwright against the creditors and trustees of the estate of Thomas Cox of Detroit. The trustees, William Macomb, George Lyons, and John Martin, had sold a tract of land that was not part of the estate. (Library and Archives Canada R9838-0-6-F, Mikan 99887, film C-11624, tome 3: Guillaume Monforton register, page 361)*

**Library and Archives Canada** holds the deceptively named "Guillaume Monforton" fonds (R9838-0-6-F, Mikan 99887), which is described as covering the period 1737 to 1796 — well before Monforton's arrival at Detroit. The fonds includes the original Monforton register as well as the following "tomes."

Film C-11624

- Tome 1, 1737–1780, is a handwritten transcription of notarial records. This transcription, as well as tomes 2, 4, 5, and 6, was made in 1886 and is different from the transcriptions at the Burton Historical Collection mentioned earlier. Tome 1 is the largest volume at well over one thousand pages. A list of notaries in the front of this volume includes Bouvard, Jean Baptiste Campeau, Philippe Dejean, Deruisseau, Gabriel Legrand, Navarre, Panet, Philibert, and Thomas Williams.
- Tome 2, 1780–1784, is a transcription of "Registre du Notaire Thomas Williams."
- Tome 3, 1786–1792, is the original Guillaume Monforton register and includes affidavits certifying its provenance. Monforton used a mixture of French and English and some items are recorded twice — once in each language.

Film C-11625

- Tome 4, 1790–1796, pages 1–133 is "Registre 4eme Français." The last entry is 21 May 1800. It is followed by "Registre 4eme Anglais," which doesn't necessarily match the French registre.

*Record of the 1768 will of Peter McIntyre "of Scotland and now in Detroit." (Library and Archives Canada R9838-0-6-F, Mikan 99887, film C-11625, tome 5: Registre No. 1 Anglais, page 13)*

- Tome 5, 1766–1780, pages 1–352 is "Registre No. 1 Anglais."
- Tome 6, 1776–1784, pages 1–460 is "Registre No. 2, Anglais." It ends with note that "this register was sent down to Quebec … in 1784, where it remained until 1789 when it was brought up from there by William Dummer Powell …"
- Tome 7 is a series of nearly alphabetical handwritten indexes to each register (six separate indexes). Some index entries include notes as to content but most are just names with page numbers. The index is in French except for last two volumes.

In his 1922 book, *The City of Detroit, Michigan, 1701–1922*,[3] Clarence M. Burton (for whom the Burton Collection was named) mentions several cases involving inheritance from these records:

- Page 175: entry from 13 March 1773, but dated 22 January 1772, Petition to Major Henry Basset, Commander at Detroit for William Edgar, James Sterling, George Meldrum, Andrews and Meldrum representing Campbell, Elice and Porteus, and P. Dejean, stating that they are the principal creditors of the estate of late Mr. and Mrs. Chabert. The "effects" are in danger of fire and theft and they ask Basset to order that the effects be sold and the proceeds be "lodged in safety," and that he order a distribution.
- Pages 175–76: two wills from the papers of Judge Charles Moran (the Judge Charles Moran papers are now in the manuscript collection of

3. Burton, Clarence M., *The City of Detroit, Michigan, 1701–1922, Volume 1* (Detroit: S.J. Clarke Publishing Company, 1922) *www.archive.org/details/cityofdetroitmic01burt*.

the Burton Historical Collection at the Detroit Public Library).

1. Will of Joseph Chapoton dated 1 March 1761, made before the royal notary at Detroit. Approved in 1776 by P. Dejean, notary.
2. Will of Madelaine Chapoton, wife of Gabriel Legrande, not dated but references ordinance of 1762. Signed by two notaries, Navarre and Jean Baptiste Campau.

- Page 176: Volume B of "old records," page 23, reference to 1769 will of Alexis Chapoton who later went to New Orleans where he died. The will was opened and declared valid by Judge Dejean in 1777. (This record is in Register B at the Wayne County Register of Deeds as noted previously.)

## ENGLISH COMMON LAW VERSUS FRENCH CIVIL LAW

With the Treaty of Paris in 1763 came English common law and the Church of England, but a special proviso kept responsibility for the probate of wills out of the hands of the Bishop of London's ecclesiastical courts and gave it to the governor of Quebec. (In England at this time, the probate of wills was handled by a maze of ecclesiastical courts depending on the location, status, and perhaps preference of the testator's family or executor.)

In estate matters, English common law and French civil law were very different.

In French civil law, a will could include both real property (the farm, for example) and chattels or moveables — like grandmother's silver candlesticks. The will came into effect on the death of the testator and it was not necessary to prove its validity in a court. However, if there was no will, the court got involved in the distribution of the estate.

English common law required the court process if the will included chattels or moveables; that is, if it was a will of *personalty*. A will that bequeathed only real property (the farm) came into effect on the death of the testator.

Practically speaking, in British North America between 1763 and the Quebec Act of 1774, both systems (French and English) operated side by side. When residents from Britain or other North American colonies died, their relatives applied to the court for letters of administration or letters probate. Very few French families went through the same process, but chose to maintain the French practice with which they were familiar. The practice in civil law, if there was no valid will, was for an officially sanctioned gathering of family and friends of the deceased person to decide who would be best to look after the estate. That person would be appointed as a *curateur* or administrator. For more insight into the difference between English and French laws and how they were used simultaneously in Quebec and Upper Canada, see the work of the Honourable William Renwick Riddell, *The Bar and the Courts of the Province of Upper Canada, or Toronto* (Toronto: MacMillan Company, 1928), 10–13; and "The Prerogative Court in Upper Canada," in *Ontario Historical Society Papers and Record, vol. XXIII* (Toronto: Ontario Historical Society, 1926), 397–412.

In 1774, the Quebec Act restored the use of French civil law for private matters — including inheritance. It was no longer necessary to obtain a grant of probate or letters of administration.

## PREROGATIVE COURTS

In 1777, Prerogative Courts were established at Quebec and Montreal to look after the formal part of the process — the gathering of family and friends to select a curateur and the court's endorsement of their choice. Rather than create a separate set of officials for the Prerogative Courts, the duties were assigned to judges of the Courts of Common Pleas.

In this early period, you can imagine just how remote the settlements at Niagara and in the Detroit/Windsor area were from Montreal. In 1788, officials made an attempt to bring government and the courts a little closer by recognizing the size of the area and dividing Western Quebec into four Districts: Luneburg, Mecklenburg, Nassau, and Hesse. Courts were established in each District, including a Prerogative Court. Again, judges of the Courts of Common Pleas (three for each District) did double duty as Prerogative Court officials.

The Prerogative Courts were also responsible for the appointment of a guardian or *tuteur* for orphaned or abandoned children, and could be called upon to appoint a curateur for an estate where the owner was known to be alive but had abandoned the property. Both tasks were also accomplished with a gathering of friends and family. These records are also of great interest to family historians.

The District Prerogative Courts were abolished in 1792.

## PREROGATIVE COURT OF HESSE DISTRICT (LATER WESTERN)

The register book of the Prerogative Court of the District of Hesse (RG 22-6 at the Archives of Ontario) is the best surviving example of how the Prerogative Courts worked. Hesse included the Detroit/Windsor area. The court sat at L'Assomption, now part of Windsor. The register covers the years 1789 to 1791, which appears to be the entire active existence of the court. All cases were confirmed by Judge William Dummer Powell.

Powell, a fluently bilingual lawyer, replaced the three men orig-inally appointed as judges in Hesse — Jacques Duperon Baby, Alexander McKee, and William Robertson — in response to a petition from area residents. The petitioners felt that while the original appointees were respected and capable, they had no legal training and, because of their involvement in trade, could not be independent. The appointees agreed and stepped aside for Powell.

The register documents the appointment of curateurs in twenty-two cases. (Remember that under civil law, this process was only required for individuals who died without a will.) In each case, one or two interested parties petitioned the judge (Powell) to set things in motion. A group of family and friends (with most relationships to the deceased identified) was gath-ered at a hearing to select the person. The curateur agreed to act and was confirmed by the court. The names of the deceased, petitioner(s), and others mentioned in each of the twenty-two cases are listed on the following pages — in my best interpreta-tion of the handwriting. The cases are listed alphabetically by the surname of the deceased.

The register at the Archives of Ontario is actually a bound photostatic copy of the original register. The Archives Descriptive Database lists the location of the original register as unknown, although it seems to have been located in the Registry Office at Chatham in the 1920s. See Riddell, William Renwick, *The Bar and the Courts of the Province of Upper Canada or Ontario* (Toronto: The MacMillan Company of Canada, 1928), 66–67. Other pho-tostatic copies of the register can be found in the Law Society of Upper Canada's Great Library and in the Burton Historical Collection at Detroit Public Library. The page numbers on the following table refer to any of the three copies.

# Early Records of Inheritance, 1763 to 1793 or Thereabouts

| Page | Deceased | Petitioner | Others Involved | Date of Application |
|------|----------|-----------|-----------------|---------------------|
| 30–31 | James Bennett of Niagara, formerly of Detroit, merchant, died summer 1786 | Nathan Williams of Detroit, merchant | George Meldrum, William Park, George Leith, Angus McIntosh, George Lyons, James May, James Abbott, David Robertson | 7 April 1791 |
| 19–20 | Joseph Bourdon (dit Labreche) of Riviere aux Raisin | Pierre Branconnin of Detroit | brother-in-law Jacques Rolland, Jacques Gagnier, Joseph Langlois, Jean Bte Bourdeaux, Jacques Granger, Louis Dragon, Hugh Heward of Detroit | 12 November 1790 |
| 1–2 | Jacques Campeau | son Jacques Campeau | 4 minors, Simon Campeau, Jean Bte Campeau, Baptiste Campeau, Guillaume St Bernard, Charles Morran, Baptiste Meloches, Baptiste Peltier | 1 July 1789 |
| 3–4 | John Casety | creditor James Fraser of Detroit, merchant | John Askin, William Robertson, John Richardson, Richard Pollard, John Martin, William Monforton, attorney Walter Roe of Detroit, Therese Baby (widow of John Casety), François Baby (brother of Therese) | 26 August 1789 |
| 31–33 | Mary Crofton of Detroit | George McDougall of Detroit, merchant | creditor Mrs. Philo Letitia Thompson of Montreal, milliner | 26 May 1791 |
| 15 | Philip Dejeane, formerly of Detroit, justice of the peace | James May of Detroit, gentleman and brother-in-law | Gregor McGregor, Jonathan Schieffelin, William Hands, Thomas Smith, Charles Smyth, James May, Jean Marie Bomrin | 8 July 1790 |

# INHERITANCE IN ONTARIO

| Page | Deceased | Petitioner | Others Involved | Date of Application |
|------|----------|------------|-----------------|---------------------|
| 22–23 | Philip Dejeane and wife | James May of Detroit (uncle of minor Pierre Dejeane) | minor Pierre Dejeane, Robert Navarre Sr. (great uncle of Pierre), François Navarre (grand cousin to Pierre), Dominique St. Cosme (uncle of Pierre), Lambert Beaubien (grand cousin to Pierre), Jancair De Chabert, Walter Roe, Antoine Beaubin (grand cousin of Pierre), Amable St. Cosme | 7 October 1790 |
| 13–14 | Charles Deforges dit St Maurice of Miamy, blacksmith | Antoine Lasalle of Detroit, merchant | brother François Deforges dit St Maurice, Charles Smyth, James May, Gregor McGregor, Alexis Maisonville, [Incain] de Charlebert, Portier Benac | 24 June 1790 |
| 12–13 | François Genié of Miamis | Gabriel Godfrey, merchant | brother Honoré Genié, Alex Bienvenue, Joseph Gouget, Pierre Durand, François Cilot, Jean Baptiste Cilot, François Pepin | 19 June 1790 |
| 17–18 | Nicolas Goyeaux | Marie Janne Peltier, widow of the deceased | Daughter Caterine Goyeaux, André Peltier (father-in-law), brother Lois Goyeaux, brother-in-law Vital Dumonchelle, Antoine Meloche (widow's uncle), François Perthui, Joseph Pouchet | 18 September 1790 |
| 16–17 | Garret Greverat of Detroit, silversmith | creditor William Groesbeck of Detroit, merchant | father-in-law Jacob Harsen, William Groesbeck (brother-in-law of Jacob Harsen), John Burrell, Alexander McKenzie, James Abbott, Charles Vallee, John Dodamead | 2 September 1790 |
| 4–5 | Samuel Judah of the City and State of New York, merchant | James Fraser of Detroit, merchant, substitute of Edward William Gray of Montreal | John Askin, William Robertson, John Richardson, Richard Pollard, John Martin, William Monforton, Walter Roe | 26 August 1789 |

# Early Records of Inheritance, 1763 to 1793 or Thereabouts

| Page | Deceased | Petitioner | Others Involved | Date of Application |
|------|----------|------------|-----------------|---------------------|
| 7–9 | Nicholas Lorrain of Miamis Town, trader | Walter Roe, attorney for James Abbott of Detroit, merchant | Widow, Jean Bte Chappaton brother-in-law to deceased, merchant William Hands of Detroit, Robert Abbott, William Christie, Alex Clerk, Thomas Smith | 1 April 1790 |
| 28–29 | John McPherson of Detroit, trader, died at River Huron near Sandusky 15 November 1790 | William and David Robertson of Detroit, merchants | Richard Pollard, John Martin, James McIntosh, Alexander McKenzie, George Ironside, William Christie, Walter Roe | 7 March 1791 |
| 24–27 | Michel Roy of Parish of Assomption (includes inventory) | Janne Viller, widow of Michel Roy | Lois Viller dit St Lois (brother of widow), Thomas Pajotte (brother-in-law of widow), François Muttons, Simon Droulliat, J Bte Antallia, Joseph Bondy, Joseph Pouget, creditors: Bondy, Baby, Meldrum, Abbott, Robertson, Christie, Martin, Trudelle, Antallia, Madame Lafond, Doctor Harffy, Pajotte | 24 February 1791 |
| 33–36 | Thomas Shepherd of Detroit, merchant, partner in firm of Leith and Shepherd | George Leith of Detroit, merchant | William Park, John Martin, David Robertson, James May, George Ironside, Nathan Williams, William Shepherd of Detroit merchant | 11 August 1791 |
| 6–7 | Joseph Socia | Son Joseph Socia, Ambroise Tremblay | 10 minors, Lois Tremblay, Joseph Tremblay, Ignace Tremblay, Ambroise Tremblay, Francois Tremblay, Gageton Segan, Baptiste Campeau | 5 November 1789 |
| 5–6 | Garret Teller | Jacob Visgar of Detroit, merchant, only relative residing in the jurisdiction | William Robertson, Walter Roe, Richard Pollard, James Fraser, John Martin, Charles Smyth | 8 August 1789 |

| Page | Deceased | Petitioner | Others Involved | Date of Application |
|------|----------|------------|-----------------|---------------------|
| 10–11 | Augustin Thèbault of Detroit, merchant | Catherine Billion dite L'Esperence, widow of the deceased | daughter Marie Catherine Thèbault, Antoine Minné (great grandfather of Marie Catherine), Michelle or Mitchel Hood, Joseph Voyer, Jean François Girardin, Jean Bte Racourt, François Xavier L'atendre | 12 April 1790 |
| 9–10 | Thomas Williams of Detroit, merchant | Cecil Campeau widow of the deceased | John Askin, William Robertson, Richard Pollard, John Richardson, John Martin, William Monforton, Joseph Campeau brother of widow Cecil, James Fraser of Detroit merchant | 26 August 1790 |
| 21–22 | Peter Younge of Rivière la Tranche, died November 1789 | Daniel Field of Detroit, blacksmith | minor son Peter Younge, Isaac Dolson of Riviere la Tranche, Daniel Fields, Amos Weston, Hezikiah Willcox, Peter Shank, Thomas Smith, Jacob Quant | 15 November 1790 |

The Honourable William Renwick Riddell describes several cases from the register in "The Prerogative Court in Upper Canada," in *Ontario Historical Society Papers and Records, vol. XXIII* (Toronto: Ontario Historical Society, 1926), 397–412.

Note that in some cases further records may be found in the records of the Hesse District Court of Common Pleas as the curateurs pursued creditors through the court to collect money owed to the estate. The minutes of the Hesse District Court of Common Pleas are at the Archives of Ontario in RG 22-5, volume 1.

# PREROGATIVE COURT OF LUNEBURG DISTRICT (LATER EASTERN)

The surviving records for the Prerogative Court of the District of Luneburg are scattered, but perhaps fairly complete considering the size of the population. I have located records for seven individuals. In contrast to Hesse, which was a very French settlement, the Luneburg records are a mixture of civil and common law. Judges active in Luneburg appear to have been Richard Duncan and John McDonell, although Edward Jessup and Alexander McDonnell were also entitled to act.[4]

The following five cases are found at the beginning of "Liber A, Register of the Surrogate Court for Eastern District of Province of Upper Canada and Johnstown." The book (Library and Archives Canada MG 9, D 14, 8) is a handwritten copy of a register that was in Brockville, commissioned by the Public Archives of Canada in 1965, and includes an index. It is also available through familysearch.org on film 477530, item 3.

| Page | Deceased | Petitioner | Others Involved | Date of Grant/ Application |
|---|---|---|---|---|
| 1–3 | Timothy Buell of the 8th township (will) | Mary Buell and Joseph McNish | William Buell, Bernsle Buell, Jonathan Buell, Samuel Peters Buell, Hannah McNish, Timothy Buell jr., Sabina Hinn | 24 January 1789 |
| 5–6 | Adam Cline of Osnabruck (administration) | Catharine Cline | Note: There is a second copy at the very end of the register, after the index. | 19 June 1790 |
| 7–8 | Barnaby Spencer of Cornwall, yeoman (appointment of curator) | Richard Wilkinson of Charlottenburg, agent for Thomas Coffin of Point du Lac | William Falkner of Lancaster, Duncan Markason of Lancaster, Murdoch McLean and Jack Summers of Charlottenburg, Daniel or David Campbell and John Smith of Cornwall and James Clark of Charlottenburg | 21 June 1790 |

4. Armstrong, Frederick H., *Handbook of Upper Canadian Chronology, revised edition* (Dundurn Press: Toronto, 1985), 116.

| Page | Deceased | Petitioner | Others Involved | Date of Grant/ Application |
|------|----------|-----------|-----------------|----------------------------|
| 9–10 | Alexander McPherson of Charlottenburg, yeoman (appointment of curator) | William Faulkner of Lancaster and John McNairn of Cornwall | Capt. John McKenzie, James McPherson, Murdoch McLean, John Cameron, Alex Cameron, John McCredy and John McKay of Charlottenburg | 2 November 1790 |
| 11–12 | Captain P Everitt of Osnabruck | Richard Wilkinson of Charlottenburg | James Gray and Thomas Swan of Cornwall, Rev. John Bethune, John McKenzie, Hugh McDonell, Chichester McDonell, Ranald McDonald or McDonell of Charlottenburg, Archibald McDonell of Osnabruck | 8 November 1791 |

A few loose pages from the minute book of the Luneburg District Prerogative Court survive in RG 22-7 at the Archives of Ontario. Four of the five cases mentioned in the previous table are also included in the following list. Subtle differences in the spellings of names might be worth pursuing.

| Deceased | Petitioner | Others Involved | Date of Grant/ Application |
|----------|-----------|-----------------|----------------------------|
| Adam Cline of Osnabrook (2 documents) | Catharine Cline | | Administration granted 19 June 1790 |
| Captain Peter Everitt of Osnabrook | Richard Wilkinson of Charlottenburg | James Gray of Cornwall, Thomas Swan of Cornwall, Rev. John Bethune, John McKenzie, Hugh McDonell, Chicester McDonell, Ranald McDonell, Archibald McDonell of Osnabrook | 8 November 1791 |
| Alexander McPherson of Charlottenburg, yeoman | William Faulkner of Lancaster, John McNairn of Cornwall | Captain John McKenzie, James McPherson, Murdoch McLean, John Cameron, Alexander Campbell, John McCredy, John McKay of Charlottenburg | |

| Deceased | Petitioner | Others Involved | Date of Grant/ Application |
|---|---|---|---|
| Barnaby Spencer of Cornwall, yeoman | Richard Wilkinson of Charlottenburg, agent for Thomas Coffin of Point du Lac, District of Montreal | William Faulkner of Lancaster, Duncan Markason of Lancaster, Murdoch McLean of Charlottenburg, Jacob Summers of Charlottenburg, Daniel Campbell of Cornwall, John Smyth of Cornwall, James Clark of Charlottenburg | 1 June 1790 |

A third handful of records for the Prerogative Court of the Luneburg District are at the Archives of Ontario in RG 22-180, Leeds and Grenville United Counties Surrogate Court filings. There are five cases that fall into the Prerogative Court era. Two have been documented in the previous lists, but the other three were not officially recorded.

| Deceased | Petitioner | Others Involved and Notes | Date of Grant/ Application |
|---|---|---|---|
| Timothy Buell | | (this file was missing in March 2012) | 1786 |
| Abijah Wead of Twp 4 (Williamsburgh) | | Un-proved and unregistered will | Will written 27 March 1786 |
| Adam Cline | Catherine Cline | Actual letters of administration with seal of the Prerogative Court of Luneburg in Province of Quebec | 1790 |
| Christian Sheek, died April 1792 | Son David Sheek of Stormont | Abraham Marsh of Stormont | November and December 1792 |
| Thomas McNight of Edwardsburg | | Undated will and oath of Thos Fraser that McNight's father-in-law should act as administrator. [States "Luningburgh County," which probably refers to Luneburg District, limiting the date to before October 1792.] | Prior to October 1792 |

*Unproven and unregistered will of Abijah Wead of Williamsburgh Township, written in 1786. (Archives of Ontario RG 22-180 Leeds and Grenville United Counties Surrogate Court filings, container 1, B231572)*

## PREROGATIVE COURT OF MECKLENBURG DISTRICT (LATER MIDLAND)

Richard Cartwright, Neil McLean, James Clark, and Clark's replacement, Hector McLean, were empowered to act as judges. The court sat in Kingston and briefly in Adolphustown.[5] I have been unable to locate any records for this court.

## PREROGATIVE COURT OF NASSAU DISTRICT (LATER HOME)

Benjamin Pawling, Peter Tenbroeck, and Nathaniel Pettit were commissioned as judges.[6] I have been unable to locate any records for this court, but Jesse Pawling seems to have dealt with at least one case in his other role as judge in the Court of Common Pleas for Nassau District. The court's minute book is preserved in the Toronto Reference Library's Baldwin Room manuscript collection.

> General Quarter Sessions of the Peace and Court of Common Pleas of Nassau District, Navy Hall, 14 October 1788, before John Butler, Robert Hamilton, and Jesse Pawling, justices:

> The Court having fully examined the last will and testament of Thomas Millard approve of it as legal. [Remainder of item is struck through.] Their opinion is that the one third of the estate is bequeathed to the Widow, and the other two thirds being not bequeathed to any person by the

---

5. Riddell, William Renwick, *The Bar and the Courts of the Province of Upper Canada or Ontario* (Toronto: The MacMillan Company of Canada, 1928), 50.
6. *Ibid.*, 51.

said will, that Mary Millard his lawful daughter is become Heir at Law to the two thirds aforesaid.

## RESEARCH TIPS FOR THIS PERIOD

• Researchers with roots in the Windsor/Detroit area before 1800 should explore notarial records. Start with the typewritten index to Registers A, B, and C at the Burton Historical Collection.

• Although they are not plentiful, the records of the prerogative courts are a great source for family relationships.

• Remember that the prerogative courts used mainly French civil law, so it was not necessary to bring an estate with a will before the court.

• Some wills seem to have been registered after the fact when the Court of Probate and District surrogate courts became available.

• Documentation of estate matters may turn up in the personal papers of later family members, friends, and business associates or legal professionals. See chapter 6.

• Inheritance of real estate may be documented in land records and in the records of the Heir and Devisee Commissions. See chapter 6.

# CHAPTER 3

## The Court of Probate, 1793 to 1858

The Court of Probate was established in 1793. At the same time, surrogate courts were set up in each District of Upper Canada. Together, they dealt with the disposition of estates and replaced the old prerogative courts that had been abolished in 1792. The Court of Probate had jurisdiction over the whole of Upper Canada. A surrogate court handled estates only within its District. The surrogate courts handled the majority of estates.

The Court of Probate had exclusive jurisdiction when the value of the estate was greater than £5 and included real property in more than one District. By today's standards, £5 sounds like an impossibly low value, and land in more than one District sounds almost unachievable. Bear in mind, though, that currency was always in short supply in Upper Canada. Land, on the other hand, was seemingly endless. Military service, public service, and even willingness to settle in a new area were rewarded with land grants — sometimes amounting to thousand of acres. Settlers with an entrepreneurial bent could accumulate additional land through family connections or they could buy it cheaply. Don't be dissuaded from looking at the Court of Probate because your ancestors were "just farmers." For more about the land granting process in Ontario, see Brenda Dougall Merriman's *Genealogy in Ontario: Searching the Records* (Toronto: Ontario Genealogical Society, 2008).

The Court of Probate was located in the provincial capital. An official principal and a registrar were appointed to oversee its operation. For a list of the appointees, see page 20 in Frederick Armstrong's *Handbook of Upper Canadian Chronology* (Toronto: Dundurn Press, 1985). The Court of Probate's province-wide jurisdiction meant that the administrator of an estate could deal with one central court rather than traipsing around to each

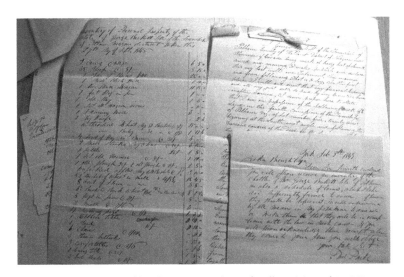

*Original 1848 estate file of George Beckett of Pelham Township, Niagara District. The estate was handled by the Court of Probate because George owned land in Niagara, Western, and Brock Districts. The will mentions that his "aged mother" Eunice should continue to be supported as specified in his "late father's will." George states that if the unborn child his wife is carrying is male, he should be called George Beckett; however, he seems to have lived longer than expected. A codicil splits baby George's inheritance with a younger brother, Ralph. The file includes an inventory. (Archives of Ontario RG 22-155 Court of Probate estate files, film MS 638-40, arranged alphabetically)*

District court. It also acted as a superior court, hearing appeals from orders or judgments of the surrogate courts.

In 1827, jurisdiction of both the Court of Probate and the surrogate courts was increased to include guardianship matters.

The Court of Probate was abolished in 1858 and replaced by an expanded and reorganized surrogate court system.

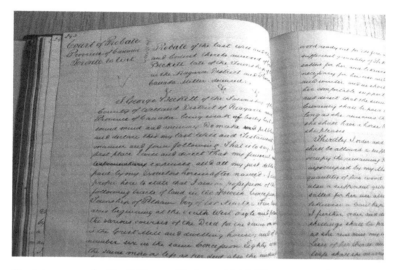

*Register copy of will of George Beckett, 1848. The register also contains the codicil and grant of probate to executor Paul Park, but not the inventory. (Archives of Ontario RG 22-154 Court of Probate registers of grants of probate and administration, register J, page 293, film MS 638-35)*

## RECORDS CREATED BY THE COURT OF PROBATE

As Ontario researchers we're very lucky that, in most cases, we can look at several documents to tell the whole story of an estate's passage through the court system. The group of documents gathered to present to the court and the documents created by the process are known as the "estate file." A copy of the will (if there was one) and a record of the court's decision about administration were recorded in a "register." The records of the Court of Probate are held at the Archives of Ontario. Most have been microfilmed and are available through interloan from the Archives of Ontario or from the Family History Library in Salt Lake City.

## Estate files
## (Archives of Ontario RG 22-155):
## 12 metres of records, 2043 files

These files of documentation accumulated by each case as it passed through the system vary in content. An estate file will include the original will if there was one. The file usually includes an application to administer the estate from a family member, friend, or creditor and an indication of whether a grant of probate or administration was issued. There will often be a financial bond, an oath that the will is genuine, an approximate value of the estate, and, if you're lucky, a detailed inventory. If the administration was contested there will usually be some documentation of that action.

Estate files for the Court of Probate are available on Archives of Ontario microfilms MS 638, Reels 37 to 72. There is an index that includes the deceased's name, residence, occupation, and the date of the application, on the interloan page of the Archives of Ontario website: *www.archives.gov.on.ca/en/microfilm/c_efile.aspx.* The index will also supply the microfilm reel number.

The files were arranged in alphabetical order by surname for filming, but the contents of the files themselves are in no particular order. I recommend making a list of each of the documents by date. Then look at them in chronological order to understand the process and the significance of each item. Be sure to pay attention to notes and numbers on the back of each document. You should find a number and date that will lead you to the corresponding entry in the register of grants of probate and administration. (See the next section.)

The estate files microfilms are available from the Archives of Ontario through any institution belonging to the interloan network — primarily public and university libraries. Order the film number from the Archives of Ontario interloan index noted previously.

Court of Probate estate files are also available through FamilySearch.org's Family History Centres around the world. Use the Archives of Ontario interloan index, and then order the matching FamilySearch.org film from the following list:

| | |
|---|---|
| Abel–Anderson, Richard | 1312317 |
| Anderson, Robert–Bailey | 1312318 |
| Bain–Beasley | 1312319 |
| Bechtel–Bowman | 1312320 |
| Bowman–Cameron, Duncan | 1312321 |
| Cameron, Hugh–Canby | 1312322 |
| Canniff–Christie, John | 1312426 |
| Christie, Robert–Crabbe | 1312427 |
| Crafts–Dennis | 1312428 |
| Dent–Earnest, George | 1312429 |
| Earnest, John–Fenton | 1312430 |
| Ferguson–Foster | 1312431 |
| Foster–Grant, Hon. Alexander | 1312432 |
| Grant, John–Hardy, John | 1312433 |
| Hardy, Samuel–Hoover | 1312434 |
| Hope–Jacob | 1312435 |
| James–Kerr | 1312854 |
| Kesler–Lewis | 1312855 |
| Leys–Mateson | 1312856 |
| Matthews–McGlashan | 1312857 |

| | |
|---|---|
| McGowan–McMurray | 1312858 |
| McNab–McVeigh | 1312859 |
| Mears–Misener | 1313807 |
| Mishaw–Muns | 1313808 |
| Munsie–Parsons | 1313809 |
| Paterson–Polly | 1312862 |
| Poole–Riddle, Ann | 1312863 |
| Riddle, John–Salmon | 1312864 |
| Salyerds–Smith, Rev. John | 1312865 |
| Smith, John David–Stephens | 1312866 |
| Sterrett–Symes | 1312938 |
| Tait–Turner, Charles | 1312939 |
| Turner, Henry–Weaver, Cyrus | 1312940 |
| Weaver, Moses–Williams, John | 1312941 |
| Williams, Rowland–Yeomans | 1312942 |
| Young–Zwick | 1313543 |

## Registers of grants of probate and administration (Archives of Ontario RG 22-154): 13 volumes, A to N

Registers were kept by the registrar of the Court of Probate as the court's copy of all grants issued. They usually include a transcription of the will, if there was one, and sometimes transcriptions of applications, oaths, bonds, inventories, etc. Most information will duplicate that of the estate file, but it will clarify the court's decision and may include tidbits such as the relationship of the administrator to the deceased.

The registers are available at the Archives of Ontario on microfilms MS 638, reels 32 to 37. There are thirteen chronological volumes. Each has a semi-alphabetical index — that is, all names beginning with a specified letter are listed together with no further alphabetization. If you've looked at the estate file, you may have noted the date, letter, and folio of the corresponding register. There is also a single alphabetical index on Archives of Ontario film MS 638, reel 32.

The registers of grants of probate and administration are not available on interloan from the Archives of Ontario. However, they are available through FamilySearch.org's network of Family History Centres. Use the following film numbers to order:

| | |
|---|---|
| Probate registers A–C 1795–1831 | 1312312 Items 2–5 |
| Probate registers D–E 1825–1842 | 1312313 |
| Probate registers F–H 1827, 1837, 1840–1847 | 1312314 |
| Probate registers J–K 1847–1852 | 1312315 |
| Probate registers L–M 1852–1856 | 1312316 |
| Probate registers M–N 1856–1858 | 1312317 |

**Registrar and surrogate clerk's correspondence (Archives of Ontario RG 22-713): 2.5 centimetres of records, thirty-one letters and notes**

This is an assorted collection of correspondence, some personal, of Court of Probate Registrar Charles Fitzgibbon. Fitzgibbon became Surrogate Clerk after 1858. The letters concerning cases in the Court of Probate are described below:

- John Edward White, Thorah Township, died December 1842 (1858 request for a copy of his will to prove that tenants Edward and Sebina Coughlin have life lease on White's property and to prevent his son from "tyrannizing" them).

- Thomas Sample, from near Toronto, died about 1834 (1850 request for a copy of his will from an Ohio lawyer representing children of the brother of Thomas Sample).

- Moore, Woodstock, died about 1849 (two 1849 letters regarding the progress of a guardianship request).

- Berford, Owen Sound, died about 1857 (February 1857 letter about the attempt to get John Wellington Berford to sign an affidavit that he was witness to the will).

- Francis Wright, Belleville area, died about 1851 (1851 request for copy of the will so it can be registered on the land allowing the purchaser to get a mortgage).

### Indentures forwarded to the Registrar of the Court of Probate (Archives of Ontario RG 22-718)

This is a small collection of some eighteen original indentures that were submitted to the Court of Probate to facilitate the granting of probate or administration in a particular case. The indentures are dated between February 1818 and April 1831. The indentures are listed individually in the Archives of Ontario's Archives Descriptive Database under RG 22-718. They are not available on interloan.

## Land grant files forwarded to the Registrar of the Court of Probate (Archives of Ontario RG 22-719)

This is a series of sixteen files to support a claim of land ownership in estate cases. The documents date from April 1798 to December 1843. Several involve United Empire Loyalists. The files are listed individually in the Archives of Ontario's Archives Descriptive Database under RG 22-719. They are not available on interloan.

## Court of Chancery orders (Archives of Ontario RG 22-715)

This is a tiny collection of three files of orders from the Court of Chancery received by the registrar of the Court of Probate. The files are listed individually in the Archives of Ontario's Archives Descriptive Database under RG 22-715. They are not available on interloan. There is more about Chancery court records in chapter 5.

## RESEARCH TIPS FOR THE COURT OF PROBATE

- Court of Probate estate files and pre-1858 surrogate court estate files are listed by name in the Archives of Ontario's Archives Descriptive Database. Go to the advanced search and select "files and items." Enter the surname and narrow the search by entering RG 22-155 in the archival reference code field. To search both Court of Probate and surrogate courts, enter RG 22 followed by an asterisk.

- Look for additional clues in Court of Probate registers.
- Documentation of estate matters may turn up in the personal papers of later family members, friends, and business associates or legal professionals. See chapter 5.
- Inheritance of real estate may be documented in land records and the records of the Heir and Devisee Commissions. See chapter 6.

# CHAPTER 4

# *The Surrogate Courts, 1793 to 1989, and More Recent Estates*

In 1793, surrogate courts were established in each District of Upper Canada to look after estate matters in that District. They worked alongside the Court of Probate, the central and superior court, to replace the old prerogative courts that had been abolished a year earlier in 1792. The intention was that estates with real property in only one District would be handled by the appropriate surrogate court, and that the Court of Probate would be reserved for estates with real property spread over a wider area. However, an estate limited to a single District could be handled by either court. The vast majority of estates were dealt with by the surrogate court system.

There would appear to have been a speedy acceptance of the surrogate court system. It used English common law instead of the prerogative court's French civil law — and would have been more familiar to many new settlers, who had been used to American courts. Some of the first few entries in the surrogate court registers may predate the court itself. For example, the 1783 will and 1785 codicil of Colin Andrews of Detroit appear in the earliest records of the Western District Surrogate Court.[7] Although there is no date on the will to indicate whether Andrews

7. Archives of Ontario, Essex County Surrogate Court estate files RG 22-311, microfilm GS 1-717, and in Western District Surrogate Court register A 1785–1825, on microfilm GS 2-35.

died before the court was established in 1793, the feebleness of his 1785 signature makes it seem quite likely.

In 1827, jurisdiction of both the Court of Probate and the surrogate courts was increased to include guardianship matters. You'll find more information about guardianship records later in this chapter.

As the population grew, the original four Districts (Eastern, Midland, Home, and Western) were split and recombined until there were a total of twenty Districts. New surrogate courts were created for each new District as it appeared. In 1849, the system of Districts was abolished and jurisdiction for matters of inheritance switched to the county level. (Prior to 1849, counties had only been used for electoral and militia organization and land registry.) In some cases, "united counties" shared a surrogate court as well as some other government offices.

Generally the old records of the District court followed a logical path to the new county surrogate court, but there are a few twists. Here is a list of the twenty Districts that existed in 1849 and the county surrogate court under which the records are now filed at the Archives of Ontario:

| 1849 District | Court Under Which Records Are Now Filed |
| --- | --- |
| Bathurst District | see Lanark County |
| Brock District | see Oxford County |
| Colborne District | see Peterborough County |
| Dalhousie District | see Carleton County |
| Eastern District | see United Counties of Stormont, Dundas, and Glengarry; and RG 22-199 Eastern District Surrogate Filings |

| | |
|---|---|
| Gore District | see Wentworth County |
| Home District | see Lincoln County for records up to 1799; for records from 1800, see York County |
| Huron District | see Huron County |
| Johnstown District | see United Counties of Leeds and Grenville |
| London District | see Middlesex County |
| Midland District | see Frontenac County and RG 22-163 Midland District Surrogate Court deposition, power of attorney and bond and related documents |
| Newcastle District | see United Counties of Northumberland and Durham |
| Niagara District | see Lincoln County |
| Ottawa District | see United Counties of Prescott and Russell |
| Prince Edward District | see Prince Edward County |
| Simcoe District | see Simcoe County |
| Talbot District | see Norfolk County |
| Victoria District | see Hastings County |
| Wellington District | see Wellington County |
| Western District | see Essex County and RG 22-313 Western District Surrogate Court minutes |

## REORGANIZATION IN 1858

There was a major reorganization of the surrogate court system in 1858 with the Surrogate Courts Act. The Court of Probate — the superior court — was abolished. That meant if a person owned land in more that one county, his or her estate had to be submitted to the surrogate court where the person was resident at the time of death.

The revamped surrogate courts were also mandated to keep more records and the format of records was to be more consistent from court to court. More records are always good news for historians!

One of the most significant changes arising from the 1858 Surrogate Courts Act was the creation of the office of the Surrogate Clerk. The Surrogate Clerk was responsible for keeping a central registry of applications for grants of probate and administration for the whole province. The purpose of the registry was to prevent duplicate grants, but today the registry can be crucial in locating an estate file from this period. More about the Surrogate Clerk's records follows later in this chapter.

From 1858 to 1989, the surrogate court system operated in more or less the same manner. New counties and, in northern Ontario, judicial districts were created to reflect a growing population, and new surrogate courts followed. New types of records were required from time to time to comply with new legislation. New officials were appointed occasionally and they reorganized the records — with varying degrees of success. The Archives of Ontario's finding aids describe many of these idiosyncrasies, but figuring out the system is part of the researcher's challenge when approaching an unknown surrogate court! For a list of the surrogate court record series for each county court, see appendix A.

In 1989, the surrogate courts were merged with High Court of Justice, the District Court, and the Civil Division of the Provincial Court to become the Ontario Court of Justice (General Division).

## RECORDS CREATED BY THE PRE-1859 SURROGATE COURTS

Most of the records of the pre-1859 surrogate courts are readily available at the Archives of Ontario. There are a couple of exceptions:

- "Liber A, Register of the Surrogate Court for Eastern District of Province of Upper Canada and Johnstown" is part of the Johnstown District Collection (MG 9, D 14, 8) at Library and Archives Canada in Ottawa. The book is a handwritten copy of a register that was in Brockville, commissioned by the Public Archives of Canada in 1965, and includes an index. It is also available through FamilySearch.org's network of Family History Centres (film 477530, item 3). A similar but not identical register is available at the Archives of Ontario on microfilm GS 2-80 or through FamilySearch.org on film 466945.

- Until 2008, many records of the London District Surrogate Court and Middlesex County Surrogate Court were held at the Regional Collection of the University of Western Ontario. They were transferred to the Archives of Ontario in 2008, but some records have not been added yet to the Archives Descriptive Database or other finding aids. However, there is a list of the items transferred on the University's Archives and Research Collections Centre website: *www.lib.uwo. ca/archives/court_records_transfers.html*. Until these records are fully described, Archives of Ontario reference staff can help you locate them.

In the name of God Amen,

I William Percival, of the Township of Oxford, in the District of Johnstown, in the Province of Canada Yeoman, being of sound and disposing mind and memory and understanding, but mindful of my mortality do this twenty sixth day of June in the Year of Our Lord One Thousand Eight hundred and forty three, Make and publish this my Last Will and Testament; in manner and form following; that is to say:

First I give and bequeath unto Susannah my Wife, her heirs and assigns, Lot Number Seven in the second Concession of the Township of Oxford aforesaid, Containing by admeasurement two hundred Acres more or less, butted and bounded as described in the government Deed of the same; to have and to hold the same, to her the said Susannah my Wife her heirs and assigns forever. I do also give and bequeath unto my Wife Susannah aforesaid, for and during the term of her natural life; or during the time she shall remain my Widow; all that parcel or tract of land situate lying and being in the first Concession of Oxford aforesaid, being composed of the North East half of Lot Number seven in the said first Concession; and from and after her decease or marriage, I give devise and bequeath the same to my son Zecharias Percival, his heirs and assigns forever: to have and to hold the said last mentioned parcel or tract of land, from

72

*The will of William Percival filed 8 February 1847 in Johnstown District Surrogate Court. Part of William Percival's estate file, the will was written in June 1843 and a codicil was added in May 1844. Although the will was not probated until 1847, the estate file includes an inventory taken 25 March 1845 — narrowing the window for William's death to between May 1844 and March 1845. Relatives mentioned in the will include William's wife, Susannah; sons Zecharias, Roger, George, and William; daughters Charlotte (wife of Walter Percival) and Mary Ann (wife of James Little). (Archives of Ontario RG 22-179 Leeds and Grenville Surrogate Court estate files, Film MS 638-28, arranged alphabetically)*

The following pre-1859 record categories are of most use for family history research.

## Estate Files

These files of documentation accumulated by each case as it passed through the system vary in content. An estate file will include the original will if there was one. The file usually includes an application to administer the estate from a family member, friend, or creditor and an indication of whether a grant of probate or administration was issued. There will often be a financial bond, an oath that the will is genuine, an approximate value of the estate, and, if you're lucky, a detailed inventory. If the administration was contested there will usually be some documentation of that action.

Estate files for the various surrogate courts are available on microfilm at Archives of Ontario. For estate files up to 1858 (and a few years later for some courts) there is a province-wide index that includes the deceased's name, residence, occupation, and the date of the application, on the Archives of Ontario website: *www. archives.gov.on.ca/en/microfilm/c_efile.aspx*. The index will also supply the microfilm reel number.

In most cases, the files were arranged in alphabetical order by surname for filming, but the contents of the files themselves are in no particular order. I recommend making a list of each of the documents by date. Then look at them in chronological order to understand the process and the significance of each item. Be sure to pay attention to notes and numbers on the back of each document. You should find a number and date that will lead you to the corresponding entry in the register of grants of probate and administration. (See the next section.)

Most of the pre-1859 surrogate court estate files microfilms are available from the Archives of Ontario through any institution belonging to the interloan network — primarily public and university libraries. Order the film number from the index noted on the previous page.

Many surrogate court estate files are also available through FamilySearch.org's Family History Centres around the world. Use the online index, then search the Family History Library Catalog on FamilySearch.org by place name (the county) and look for the "probate records" classification. The Archives of Ontario has a conversion list on the interloan page of its website to help convert an Archives of Ontario film number to the equivalent "GSU" number. (GSU stands for Genealogical Society of Utah, an old name for FamilySearch.org.) Here's the address of the conversion list: *www.archives.gov.on.ca/en/microfilm/c_gsuconversion.aspx*.

## Registers of Grants of Probate and Administration

Registers were kept by the registrars of the various surrogate courts as the court's chronological copy of all grants issued. They usually include a transcription of the will, if there was one, and sometimes transcriptions of applications, oaths, bonds, inventories, and so on. Most information will duplicate that of the estate file, but it will clarify the court's decision and may include tidbits such as the relationship of the administrator to the deceased. Unlike the estate files, the register will present the story of the file's progress through the court in chronological order.

There can be significant differences in the spelling of the name in the register and the estate file. For instance, in the Eastern District Surrogate Court register, the 1819 administration of Peter Bresee of Bastard Township is recorded. Mr. Bresee's estate file consists of an inventory filed under the name "Burser" — not a variation that would easily come to mind!

Pre-1859 registers for most surrogate courts are available at the Archives of Ontario on microfilm, although there are significant gaps for some counties. The style varies from court to court, but they usually include a semi-alphabetical index — that is, all names beginning with a specified letter are listed together with no further alphabetization. Be wary that some letters of the alphabet may be further refined in the index; for instance, names beginning with *Mc*. If you've already looked at the estate file, you may have noted the date, letter, and folio of the corresponding register.

Some of the pre-1859 registers are available on interloan from the Archives of Ontario. Check the interloan page to see what is available for your county. Others may be available through FamilySearch.org's network of Family History Centres. Search the Family History Library Catalog by place name (the county) and look for the "probate records" classification. The registers are identified as "records" rather than registers. The Archives of Ontario has a conversion list on the interloan page of its website to help convert an Archives of Ontario film number to the equivalent "GSU" or FamilySearch.org number. Here's the link: *www.archives.gov.on.ca/en/microfilm/c_gsuconversion.aspx*.

**Name Indexes**

Surrogate court registrars may have created a variety of indexes — to names of the deceased, executors, administrators, and such. These may be a single list or two lists divided into grants of probate and grants of administration, but it boils down to the fact that court registrars had to be able to find the records if they were asked to provide a copy. The indexes will each be a little different and will require some patience until you figure them out. The information in the Archives of Ontario's Archives

Descriptive Database and on the interloan pages — or in the Surrogate Court User's Guide at the Archives of Ontario reading room — is invaluable. Be sure to read it carefully. For estates dated earlier that 1859, start with the name index on the Archives of Ontario interloan page (mentioned previously under "Estate Files"): *www.archives.gov.on.ca/en/microfilm/c_efile.aspx*.

## Minute Books

These are not available for every court, but minute books record the cases that were presented to the court at each sitting. They are a brief record of the court's activity, but may state who was present, providing insight into delays, appointment of alternate administrators, and other details. Minute books are well worth a look to help complete the story, if they happen to have survived for your county and time period. Check appendix A to see if minute books are available for your county.

## Surrogate Court Filings

These "filings" are documents (often wills or applications for administration) that were submitted to the court but for some reason no grant of probate or administration was issued. These are small collections, but vital for the estates covered. There are pre-1859 filings at the Archives of Ontario for the following courts: Brant County, Eastern District, Frontenac County, Hastings County, Lambton County, Lanark County, Leeds and Grenville United Counties, Lincoln County, Northumberland and Durham United Counties, Perth County, Simcoe County, Welland County, and Wentworth County. The individual cases are listed by name in the Archive of Ontario's Archives Descriptive Database.

## RECORDS CREATED BY THE POST-1858 SURROGATE COURTS

Broadly drawn, the Archives of Ontario has custody of all surrogate court records more than forty years old. A new accrual of records comes to the Archives of Ontario each year. Estate files, registers, and other records needed to locate estate files are on microfilm up to 1930. The indexes created by each court are available up to 1967 on microfilm. (Many of these records are also available on interloan from the Archives of Ontario and through FamilySearch.org.)

Estate files later than 1930 (but older than forty years) have not been microfilmed, but can be requested from offsite

*Succession duty affidavit listing three relatives from the estate file of Lee Wai, laundryman of New Liskeard, 1913. (Archives of Ontario RG 22-369 Temiskaming District Surrogate Court estate files, grant 4, film MS 1443, item 2)*

storage and viewed at the Archives of Ontario. Allow a couple of days for the files to be delivered. If you can't get to the Archives of Ontario to view the paper files, you can order a copy for a fee.

Estate files less than forty years old are still held at the local courthouse (Superior Court of Justice — Estates Division). You can view the files onsite or order a copy for a fee. You will find a list of addresses for the courthouses here: *www.archives.gov.on.ca/en/microfilm/c_courts.aspx*.

Of course, there are exceptions to the way things are supposed to work. Here are some of the most important:

- For various reasons, not all estate files older than forty years have been transferred to the Archives of Ontario. For example, in the case of a small court where few estates are processed, the transfer may be held until a container is filled.
- The original estate files for Prince Edward County from 1859 to about 1968 are on loan to the Prince Edward County Archives in Picton.
- The estate files for York County up to 1967 have been microfilmed and are available at the Archives of Ontario.
- There is a very significant and inconvenient gap between the end of the indexes to estate files at the Archives of Ontario — 1967 — and the latest accrual of records — from about 1973. For this period, you'll have to contact the courthouse for the index, although the estate file itself is likely in the custody of the Archives of Ontario. Contact Archives of Ontario reference staff to confirm the location.

Post-1858 records are more detailed and plentiful than the earlier surrogate court records. The following are some of the more important categories.

## Estate Files

These files of documentation accumulated by each case as it passed through the system vary in content. The contents of post-1858 estate files become more standard. The original will is included if there was one. There will be a petition to administer the estate from a family member, friend, or creditor, and an indication of whether a grant of probate or administration was issued. There will often be a financial bond, an oath that the will is genuine, an approximate value of the estate, and a copy of the notice to the Surrogate Clerk. After 1892, wealthier estates will include detailed inventories and a list of heirs as required by the Succession Duty Act. If the administration was contested, there will usually be some documentation of that action.

Estate files up to 1931 for the various surrogate courts are available on microfilm at Archives of Ontario. Rather than the alphabetical arrangement of the pre-1859 files, post-1858 files are listed chronologically by a file number. Depending on the court, the file number may be the grant number, application number, or non-contentious business number. Knowing which one to note for your court is crucial. That information can be found in the Archives of Ontario finding aids. Use the archival reference code for the appropriate court from appendix A.

As with the earlier surrogate court files, the contents of the files themselves are in no particular order. I recommend making a list of each of the documents by date. Then look at them in chronological order to understand the process and the significance of each item. Be sure to pay attention to notes and numbers on the back of each document. You should find a number and date that will lead you to the corresponding entry in the register of grants of probate and administration (see below).

Most of the estate files up to 1931 are available on microfilm from the Archives of Ontario through interloan. Many estate files are also available through FamilySearch.org's Family History Centres around the world. Search the Family History Library Catalog on FamilySearch.org by place name (the county) and look for the "probate records" classification. Use the Archives of Ontario conversion list on the interloan page of its website to help convert an Archives of Ontario film number to the equivalent "GSU" or FamilySearch.org number. Here's the link: *www.archives.gov.on.ca/en/microfilm/c_gsuconversion.aspx*.

## Name Indexes

There are three types of indexes available for most post-1858 surrogate courts.

- *Original indexes:* Surrogate court registrars may have created a variety of indexes — to the names of the deceased, executors, administrators, and others. Court registrars had to be able to find the records if they were asked to provide a copy. The indexes will all be a little different and will require some patience until you figure them out. Consult appendix A to see what indexes are available for your court. The information in the Archives Descriptive Database and on the interloan pages — or in the Surrogate Court User's Guide at the Archives of Ontario reading room — is invaluable. Be sure to read it carefully.

- *Published indexes:* Genealogical and historical societies and individual authors have been indexing and extracting Ontario estate records for many decades. Most counties have a volume covering from 1858 to 1900, but some have more. See appendix B for a list of titles arranged by county.
- *Surrogate Clerk's records:* These records, created to avoid duplicate applications for probate or administration, can also work as a province-wide index. Read on for further information.

## Registers of Grants of Probate and Administration

Registers were kept by the registrars of the various surrogate courts as the court's chronological copy of all grants issued. They usually include a transcription of the will, if there was one, and transcriptions of applications, oaths, bonds, inventories, and so on. Most information will duplicate that of the estate file, but it will clarify the court's decision.

## Minute Books

These are not available for every court or time period, but minute books record the cases that were presented to the court at each sitting. They are a brief record of the court's activity, but may indicate who was present and provide insight into delays, appointment of alternate administrators, and so on.

## Surrogate Court Filings

These "filings" are documents (often wills or applications for administration) that were submitted to the court but for some reason no grant of probate or administration was issued. These are small collections, but vital for the estates covered. There are post-1858 filings at the Archives of Ontario for the following courts: Brant County, Essex County, Frontenac County, Hastings County, Lambton County, Lanark County, Leeds and Grenville United Counties, Lincoln County, Norfolk County, Northumberland and Durham United Counties, Ontario County, Perth County, Peterborough County, Simcoe County, Welland County, Wellington County. The individual cases have been listed in the Archive of Ontario's Archives Descriptive Database.

## Non-Contentious Business Books

In these books, the registrars recorded all applications made to the court for grants of probate or administration, whether or not a grant was issued. They include the name and residence of the deceased, date of death, and name of the person applying for a grant. A number links back to the estate file. If a caveat was filed, it will be noted.

## Grant Books

These volumes list all grants of probate and administration issued in chronological order. They include the name and residence of the deceased, date of death, and name of the person applying for a grant. A number usually links back to the estate file.

## Contentious Estate Files, Action and Matter Files

If there was a dispute about an estate, it could be resolved with a civil suit in the surrogate court. These are the resulting case files.

## Caveat Books or Caveat Files

A caveat is a document filed with the court to prevent it from issuing a grant of probate or administration without first notifying the person who filed the caveat.

## Administration Bond Books

The administrator of an estate had to provide security in the form of a bond that he or she would perform the task, and this was recorded in a bond book.

## Surrogate Clerk's Records (RG 22-514)

These are useful records if you don't know in which county surrogate court an estate was handled. The 1858 Surrogate Courts Act created the office of the Surrogate Clerk. The Surrogate Clerk was responsible for maintaining a central registry of applications for grants of probate and administration for the whole province. The purpose of the registry was to prevent duplicate grants.

The surrogate courts were required to notify the Surrogate Clerk's office of every application for a grant. The Clerk checked that no other application for that particular estate had been received, then added the application to a book and indexed it. (The applications and indexes were separate books

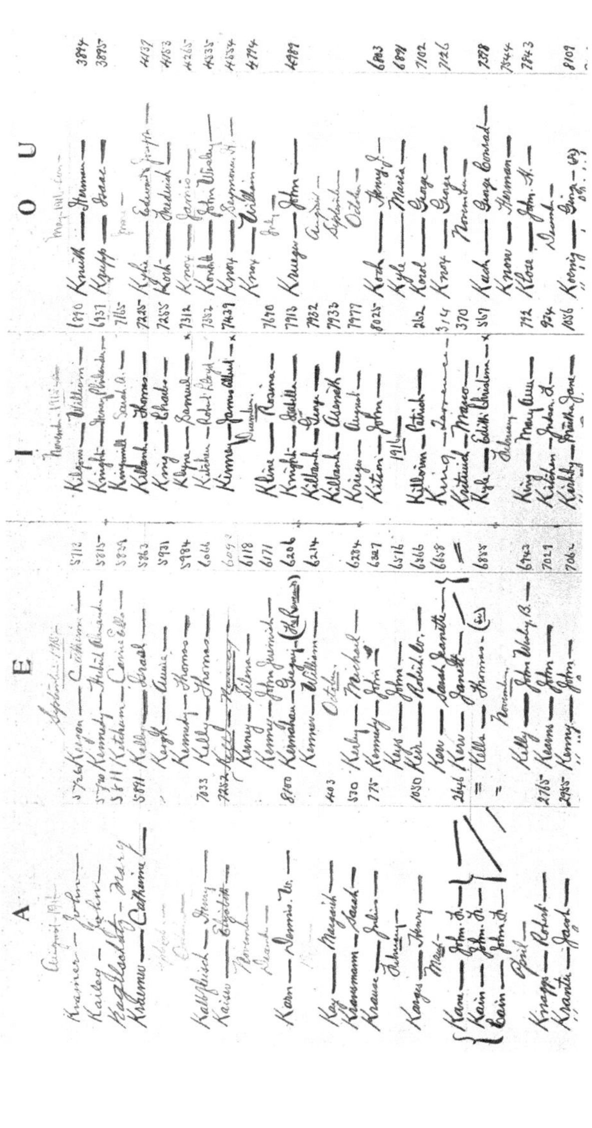

The Surrogate Clerk's index to applications for grants of probate and administrations for names beginning with K. The semi-alphabetical index uses separate columns to further divide the names by first vowel (more or less). This page covers roughly autumn 1915 to early 1917. Follow the number to the right of each name to the "notice of application" in the application register. See next image. (Archives of Ontario RG 22-514 Surrogate Clerk for Ontario applications for probate books and indexes, film MS 404-4)

*The Surrogate Clerk's application register, arranged numerically, includes deceased's name, residence, occupation or marital status, death date, name and residence of applicant, occupation, and, most importantly, the court where the application was made. Once the court is known, you can consult its index to find the estate file. (Archives of Ontario RG 22-514 Surrogate Clerk for Ontario applications for probate books and indexes, film MS 404-16)*

until 1964. They were combined in 1965.) The 98 volumes, covering 1858 to 1982, are available on microfilm at the Archives of Ontario and through interloan. See the Archives of Ontario's interloan page for a listing: *www.archives.gov.on.ca/en/microfilm/index.aspx*.

Please note that while this is a province-wide index, it will only direct you to the correct county surrogate court. You'll need to consult the records of that court to search for the estate file number. It is much more efficient to go directly to the court if you know it.

## Guardianships

In 1827, jurisdiction of both the Court of Probate and the surrogate courts was increased to include guardianship matters. The court could appoint guardians for orphaned minor children. A guardian might also be appointed if there was an inheritance to be managed for minor children — even if the mother was living. If the parent appointed a guardian or trustee in his or her will, the court procedure was not needed. The majority of orphaned children were cared for by family and friends without any formal court procedure.

From 1827 to 1858, guardianship cases for most courts can be found in the online name indexes to the Court of Probate and the surrogate courts on the Archives of Ontario's interloan page: *www.archives.gov.on.ca/en/microfilm/c_efile.aspx*. They are indexed by the name of the children.

The various surrogate courts continued to handle guardianships after 1858, but whether the records were interfiled from estate files or kept as a separate series seems to vary widely from court to court. Please see the list of archival records series in appendix A.

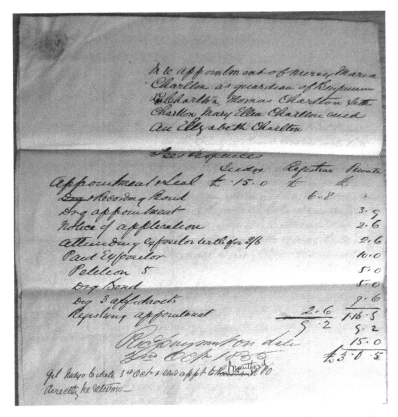

*Statement of fees for the appointment of Mercy Maria Charlton as guardian of her children, Benjamin, Thomas, Seth, Mary Ellen, and Ann Elizabeth Charlton, 1855. The guardianship file includes a petition from Mercy, the widow of the late Michael Charlton who is "best entitled," a copy of the notice published in the Brantford* Expositor, *and a £1,500 bond to be paid to the children if Mercy fails to act in their best interests until they become of age. (Archives of Ontario RG 22-325 Brant County Surrogate Court estate files, film MS 920-1, filed alphabetically)*

## RESEARCH TIPS FOR SURROGATE COURTS

- Surrogate court estate files up to 1858 are listed by name in the Archives of Ontario's Archives Descriptive Database. Go to the advanced search and select "Files and Items." Enter the surname and narrow the search by entering RG 22 followed by an asterisk in the archival reference code field. (This will also find estate files for the Court of Probate.) To search a specific court, enter the full archival reference code.
- Check appendix B for name indexes for your county.
- Every court's indexing is a little different. Be sure to consult the Archives of Ontario's finding aids for help in figuring them out.
- Documentation of estate matters may turn up in the personal papers of later family members, friends, and business associates or legal professionals. See chapter 6.
- Inheritance of real estate may be documented in land records and the records of the Heir and Devisee Commissions. See chapters 5 and 6.

# CHAPTER 5

## *Records of Inheritance in the Land Registry Office*

Although the records of the courts described in the earlier chapters of this book are the first place you should look for estate records, in fact, thousands of wills in Ontario came into effect without going anywhere near the court system. And it was all perfectly legal.

As mentioned in Chapter 2, Early Records of Inheritance, both French civil law and English common law allowed wills involving only real property to come into effect on the death of the testator. Unless the will stipulated that the property was to be sold and the proceeds distributed to the heirs (or had other complicating factors), there was no need to go through the expensive probate process. A simple transfer of ownership from the deceased to his widow or child meant the will could be registered in the land registry office.

A large collection of land registry office records has been microfilmed by FamilySearch.org. The films are available through its network of Family History Centres and most of the same films are at the Archives of Ontario designated as RG 61. The film listing for RG 61 must be consulted in person in the Archives of Ontario reading room. Note that this collection is huge, but not comprehensive. You may need to visit the local land registry office to see specific records for your area of interest.

With the reorganization and automation of the land records system in Ontario that began in the 1990s, many original documents have been relocated to local archives. Consult the local genealogical or historical society to find out if that is the case for your county.

## ABSTRACT INDEXES

*Abstract index page for Concession 1, Lot 2, Saugeen Township, Bruce County. A similar page was created for every parcel of land in Ontario. This particular page shows examples of three records of inheritance. The first, instrument 3875, is the 1893 registration of the will of Peter Hoover, which is recorded in the copybook of wills (see next illustration). Instrument 8370 shows that Henry Hoover's will was probated in the surrogate court, and instrument 8231 shows Henry's executors selling the land. (Archives of Ontario, RG 61-3 Bruce County Land Registry Office, Walkerton, Abstract index for Saugeen Township, vol. 1, film GSU 172176)*

Most Ontario land records are organized by location. Abstract indexes were created in 1865 to provide chronological summaries of the transactions relating to each parcel of property. Each page in the abstract index is designated for a single property. Starting with the grant from the Crown (or the first sale of a subdivision), each transfer, mortgage, or other document affecting the land is listed. These documents, or "instruments" as they are called in this circumstance, can include wills, quit claims or releases, and vesting orders from the Court of Chancery. An instrument number in the abstract index leads you to an original document (on microfilm at the local land registry office) or to a transcription of the document in the microfilmed Copybooks of Deeds at the Archives of Ontario or through FamilySearch.org.

*The transcription of the will of Peter Hoover, noted as instrument 3875 in the abstract index for Concession 1, Lot 2, Saugeen Township (see previous illustration). The transcription is in the copybook of deeds. (Archives of Ontario, RG 61-3 Bruce County Land Registry Office, Walkerton, Copybook for Saugeen Township, vol. E, page 175, film GSU 1722798)*

## WILLS

Until 1864, wills registered in the land registry office would be recorded with all other instruments in the Copybooks of Deeds. The instruments were entered in chronological order as they were registered — not necessarily the date the instrument was created. A will might not be registered on the property until it was necessary to prove ownership before a sale or mortgage. This could be a matter of years, or even decades. From 1865, registrars were required to create separate General Registers for the recording of wills.

*A transcription of the will of Robert Edge of the Township of Bentinck in the General Register. The will was written in March 1862, and recorded in January 1864. (Archives of Ontario, RG 61-16 Grey County North Land Registry Office, Owen Sound, General Register, Wills vol. 15, film GSU 172013)*

## QUIT CLAIMS AND RELEASES

A quit claim, or release, documents that one of the owners of a parcel of land has agreed to let it be sold or otherwise transferred. In many cases, it will be one of several family members who have inherited the land jointly. These can be particularly informative, stating relationships, addresses, and how the person came to inherit.

## COURT OF CHANCERY

The Court of Chancery was established in 1837 and until 1881 had jurisdiction over many matters concerning land, including trusts, the partition of estates, mortgages, dower, and alimony. A vesting order from the Court of Chancery listed in the abstract index is relatively rare, but it indicates that there was some dispute about the ownership of the land — usually inheritance.

Many records of the Court of Chancery are at the Archives of Ontario. Equity civil suits case files (RG 22-409) are a particularly easy-to-access source within the Chancery records. Some four thousand case files from 1869 to 1877 are listed by surname in the Archives Descriptive Database.

To see all the Archives of Ontario holdings for the Court of Chancery, search by Record Creator BA37 in the Archives Descriptive Database.

## RESEARCH TIPS FOR ESTATE RECORDS IN LAND REGISTRY RECORDS

- Search the appropriate court records first. If you don't find an estate file, then try land records.

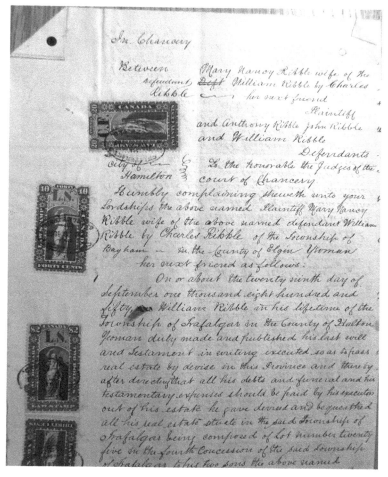

*An 1869 case file from the Court of Chancery in which Mary Nancy Ribble is complaining that her £125 legacy from the estate of her father William Ribble, who died in 1862, is overdue. It was to be paid in five annual installments by her brothers Anthony and John. (Archives of Ontario RG 22-409 Equity civil suits case files, Ribble v Ribble, box B125219)*

- A will noted in the abstract index may also have been proven in court.
- A will may be registered a considerable time after the death of the testator when the heirs want to sell or mortgage the property.
- Although the land registry system was set up in 1795, registration of land transactions was not compulsory until 1846, and abstract indexes were not created until 1865.
- For detailed information about researching in land registry records, see *Ontario Land Registry Office Records: A Guide* by Fawne Stratford-Devai and Ruth Burkholder (Global Heritage Press: Milton, ON, 2012).

# CHAPTER 6

## Other Records of Inheritance

### PROBATE RECORDS IN OTHER JURISDICTIONS

Once you've searched the various Ontario court records for a record of your ancestor's estate and come up empty-handed, consider that it may have passed through the courts in a very different jurisdiction.

For example, there are approximately 250 Ontario wills that were handled by the Prerogative Court of Canterbury in England prior to 1859. Some were prominent, even titled, individuals who may have had substantial land holdings in Britain as well as in Ontario. Others are listed as yeomen, merchants, gentleman, army officers, and other occupations that wouldn't bring to mind landed gentry status. If the person's executors or administrators were living in England, it may have been much easier to handle the estate there rather than to empower an attorney in Ontario. It almost certainly would have been faster.

A very useful index to all Prerogative Court of Canterbury wills is available on The National Archives (TNA) website: *www.nationalarchives.gov.uk/records/wills-and-probate.htm*. Digitized copies of the wills are available for a fee from TNA through its website. The wills have also been microfilmed and are available through FamilySearch.org.

Scottish wills and testaments (up to 1925 at present) are indexed on the website ScotlandsPeople (*scotlandspeople.gov.uk*). It is difficult to narrow the search to Ontario residents, but the index shows some 1,810 records from Canada. Like the Prerogative Court of Canterbury, some are for prominent people with obviously strong property connections to Scotland, but many others are not. For instance, an inventory for one Moses Staunton, a "paper stainer" from Toronto, who died in Toronto on 3 October 1877, was recorded in the Edinburgh Sheriff Court on 9 April 1878. You can search the Wills and Testaments index for free at *www.scotlandspeople.gov.uk/search/testament/index.aspx*. Digitized copies can be downloaded for a fee from the same site. Most have also been microfilmed and are available through FamilySearch.org.

When looking for inheritance records for your Ontario ancestor, broaden your search geographically. Where did the person live before coming to Ontario? Did he or she live in a different part of Canada or the United States for a time where they might have acquired land or other property? Did their children or siblings who might serve as administrators move away from Ontario?

The indexes to English and Scottish wills mentioned above are exceptional in that they cover the majority of records in those countries and contain enough details to identify places of residence. Most probate records from other jurisdictions are organized on a provincial, state, or county level, and it is only possible to search the specific jurisdiction. But if you haven't found your ancestor's records in Ontario, it could be well worth the search.

## NEWSPAPERS

Ontario newspapers carried information about estate matters for several reasons. Legal notices could be required (or desirable) at various stages of the court process. The judge could require that an advertisement be placed to locate a missing will.[8] In the case of an estate where there were no known next of kin, notices of an application for probate or administration would be published in newspapers as specified by the judge.[9] Under some circumstances, such as an application for "ancillary" probate when the will had been proven in a foreign court, notices were required to be published in the *Ontario Gazette*. The *Ontario Gazette* is an official government publication. Issues since January 2000 are available online at *www.ontariogazette.gov.on.ca*. For earlier issues, print and microfilm collections are available at major public and university libraries. Notices of applications for guardianship were also published in local newspapers. An executor could cover all of his or her bases by publishing, in the local newspaper, a time-limited notice to creditors to come forward.[10]

The details of a prominent or wealthy person's will were fine fodder for Ontario newspaper readers, even better if the deceased was a bit eccentric and the will unusual. In general, the information was published shortly after the case had progressed through the court. It was quite common to see a list of heirs and precisely what they had inherited.

Many libraries and archives in Ontario have collections of local newspapers, mostly on microfilm. The best, centralized collection of Ontario newspapers is at the Archives of Ontario, and the best collection of Toronto newspapers is at the Toronto Reference Library. For all Ontario, it is worth checking two major Toronto newspapers — the *Toronto Star* and the *Globe* (under various titles through the years). These have been digitized and can be searched online for a fee. Many public and university libraries provide free access. A number of newspapers for smaller communities have been digitized and are available through *www.ourontario.ca*. Consult local

8. Howell, Alfred, *Probate, Administration, and Guardianship: Common Form and Contentious Business* (Toronto: Carswell Co., 1895), 180–81.
9. Cowan, John, *Surrogate Court Rules of Ontario* (Toronto: Dudgeon and Thornton, 1916), 9.
10. Cowan, 73.

## Notice.

ALL perfons indebted to the Eftate of the late *James Cumming*, late of Hallowell, derceafed, are requefted to call without delay, and fettle the fame with Mr. JAMES McGREGOR, now in charge of the eftablifhment, at Hallowell bridge ;—and thofe who have claims againft the faid eftate, are defired to prefent them for adjuftment.

The ftock in Trade of the deceafed, confifting of a very complete affortment of Goods well laid in, and very fuitable to the Country, is now felling off at prices fo low, as will defervedly claim the attention of the public.

Cafh or Country produce will be taken in payment, and a credit of 6 months given to refponfible Farmers, or others.

JOHN CUMMING.
WM. MITCHELL. } Executors

Kingfton, Oct 27, 1817. 32

THE notice of a difcontinuance of the Partnerfhip between *Thorner & Moran*, figned by Mr. Thorner, and inferted in the Kingfton Gazette, was publifhed without the confent of the fubfcriber, who, in order to prevent any miftake, thinks himfelf bound to inform the public, that, altho' a diffolution of faid partnerfhip has been mentioned, it is not definitively arranged. MICHL. MORAN.

Kingfton, April 20, 1818. 47

## Notice.

THE partnerfhip mentioned a few months fince, between *Thorner, & Moran*, ceafed on 3d April, 1818. As no papers have been figned to confirm

## HATS.

SMITH & BUTTERWORTH,

RETURN their fincere thanks to their friends and the public in general, for the liberal encouragement that they have received fince they recommenced the *Hatting Bufinefs*. They have an extenfive affortment of

Ladies and Children's BONNETS, of various colors and fhapes.

Gentlemen's Beaver & fine Caftor HATS,

Likewife, Knapt and Wool Hats.

Which they will fell very low for cafh or approved credit.

Produce taken in payment.

Jan. 2. 32tf.

## Public Notice.

THE Subfcribers, Executors to the Eftate of *Charles Stuart*, Efquire, deceafed, late Sheriff of the Midland Diftrict, hereby requests all thofe indebted to the faid Eftate to make immediate payment to the faid Executors ; and all thofe who have demands againft the Eftate are requested to produce the fame duly attefted, in order that a Settlement of the Eftate may be effected as fpeedily as poffible after the firft day of July 1818.

GEORGE O. STUART,
ALLAN McLEAN, } Execu-
tors.

Kingfton, Auguft 11, 1817.—32tf

## ADVERTISEMENT.

The fubfcriber offers for Sale the

*Notices from the executors of James Cumming and of Charles Stuart appear in this detail from the* Kingston Gazette *(5 May 1818, page 4) with the purpose of clearing up any outstanding debts. From the Cumming notice we also learn that a James McGregor is now in charge of the "establishment." (Kingston Frontenac Public Library collection accessed via* ourontario.ca*)*

genealogical and historical societies to find out what is currently available for your area.

## HEIR AND DEVISEE COMMISSIONS

The records created by the two Heir and Devisee Commissions can be very significant if your ancestors were in Ontario by about 1800. Many recipients of grants of Crown land did not take the step of getting the letters patent that would finalize the transfer of ownership. In some cases the grantee had died or had transferred ownership to family members or others. To clarify titles and settle disputes, the government set up two Heir and Devisee Commissions. The commissions held hearings where the proof of ownership was presented. And of course the proof was usually very rich genealogical information.

Most of the records of the First Heir and Devisee Commission (1795–1805) are at Library and Archives Canada, under archival reference number R10875-8-2-E, with microfilm copies at the Archives of Ontario. The Archives of Ontario holds additional related material. To see all the applicable archival series at the Archives of Ontario, search the Archives Descriptive Database by creator code BA121. Indexes to the First Heir and Devisee Commission have been compiled by Linda and Gary Corupe, under the title *From Settler to Land Owner*. Seven volumes are available for purchase at this time from *www.lindacorupe.com*.

The records of the Second Heir and Devisee Commission (1805–1896) are at the Archives of Ontario. To see all the applicable archival series, search the Archives Descriptive Database by creator code BA142. The most interesting series for family history is RG 40-5. This series consists of more than five thousand case files of supporting documentation that was created for each of the cases that came before the commission.

## Notice

Take notice that James Shea of the township of Ops in the County of Victoria yeoman and Mary Dorgan wife of Michael Dorgan now residing in the State of Michigan one of the United States of America will claim before the Heir and Devisee Commissioners at the sittings to be held on the first Monday in July in the year 1874 the following parcel of Land that is to say — The East Half of the North Half of Lot number Eight in the Fifth Concession of the township of Ops in the County of Victoria Containing by admeasurement Fifty Acres be the same more or less

And take notice that the said James Shea claims an estate pur autre vie during his mother's life in said parcel and an estate in fee simple in remainder in four fifths of said parcel of land as one of the Heirs at law of his brother John Shea deceased who died unmarried and intestate in or about the month of January 1863 and who was the devisee of Edmund Shea deceased of said parcel of Land

And also as the Assignee of Ellen Shea the widow of Edward Shea deceased and mother of the said John Shea deceased

And also as Assignee of Patrick Shea, Stephen Shea, and Thomas Shea, the brothers of the said John Shea deceased.

And take notice that the said Mary Dorgan claims an estate in fee simple in remainder on the death of her mother the said Ellen Shea in an undivided one fifth part

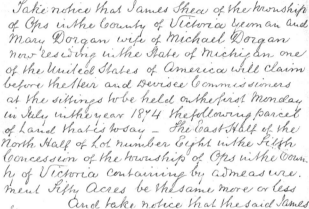

*From Second Heir and Devisee Commission case file number 40-4837, this is the 1874 public notice that James Shea and Mary Dorgan (wife of Michael Dorgan) intend to claim a fifty-acre lot in Ops Township that had belonged to their father, Edmund Shea. The file also mentions their mother, Ellen née Ryan (deceased), and siblings John (died 1862), Patrick, Stephen, and Thomas. The file includes a copy of Edmund's will. (Archives of Ontario RG 40-5 Second Heir and Devisee Commission case file 40-4837, film MS 657-93)*

These files (RG 40-5) are indexed in the Second Heir and Devisee Commission Database available on the Archives of Ontario website — leading to microfilmed case files available at the Archives of Ontario or through FamilySearch.org. Be aware that the files are indexed by the name of the person claiming ownership (the heir or devisee) whose surname may be different than the original owner. A further caution to note is that while a case file may include the names of multiple heirs, all names may not be included in the index. Don't rule out a case file because the index doesn't contain the name of your ancestor, if the names of his siblings or other possible relatives are present. Search creatively and check the original.

## MANUSCRIPT COLLECTIONS

Copies of wills and other documents frequently appear in the papers of individuals and families held in various archives and libraries around the province. The creator of the papers may have served as executor, or was an heir of the estate involved. In most cases, these documents will also appear in the applicable court records mentioned in previous chapters, but you might find working copies and drafts that tell a little more of a story than the "official" documents. A collection of documents from different eras may show the changing ownership of a piece of property.

Collections of papers that belonged to a lawyer or law firm can also be a great source. They might include wills that were never probated, as well as notes on cases in progress.

Check for manuscript collections at archives in the local area where your ancestors lived, as well as the large collections at the Archives of Ontario and Library and Archives Canada. Look beyond your direct family to neighbours and business associates who might have had an interest in the estate.

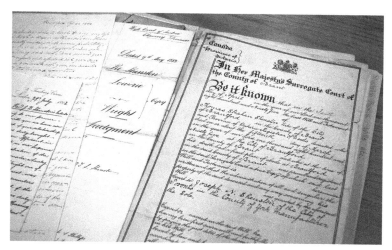

*A file of wills and associated letters from the Thomas Strahan Shenston papers. The file includes records for Benjamin Shenston of St. Catharines (circa 1861), Mary Ann Shenston (circa 1877), William Henry Shenston of Ellenboro, Wisconsin (circa 1880), and Reverend John Brittain Shenston of England (circa 1881), as well as Thomas Strahan Shenston of Brantford (circa 1895). (Toronto Reference Library, Baldwin Room manuscript collection, fonds S119)*

# APPENDIX A

## Surrogate Courts Archival Series Numbers

The Archives of Ontario has designated several archival series numbers for each county (or united counties) and each northern Ontario surrogate court. Here is an alphabetical list by county. The prefix RG 22 indicates that all series are a part of court records. You find more information about each series, including dates covered, in the Archives Descriptive Database.

**Algoma District:** RG 22-331 indexes; RG 22-332 guardianship register and bond book; RG 22-333 caveat book; RG 22-334 process book; RG 22-360 estate files; RG 22-381 guardianship files; RG 22-1045 audit book; RG 22-1046 non-contentious business book; RG 22-1047 registers; RG 22-1048 administration books; RG 22-1049 contentious estate files; RG 22-542 action and matter files.

**Brant County:** RG 22-1148 infant custody applications; RG 22-1173 executors order books; RG 22-1174 administration bond books; RG 22-1175 action and matter files; RG 22-1177 guardianship registers; RG 22-1178 general index; RG 22-323 non-contentious business books; RG 22-324 grant books; RG 22-325 estate files; RG 22-326 filings; RG 22-327 guardianship files; RG 22-373 registers.

**Bruce County:** RG 22-283 indexes; RG 22-284 registers; RG 22-285 guardianship files; RG 22-358 estate files; RG 22-1220 non-contentious business and grant book; RG 22-1221 order book; RG 22-1222 caveat book; RG 22-1223 process book; RG 22-1224 guardianship book; RG 22-1227 passing of accounts register; RG 22-1228 passing of accounts records.

**Carleton County:** RG 22-224 registers; RG 22-225 non-contentious business and grant books; RG 22-354 estate files, RG 22-1360 procedure books; RG 22-1361 order books; RG 22-1362 guardianship files; RG 22-1363 grant books; RG 22-1365 contentious estate files.

**Cochrane District:** RG 22-370 estate files; RG 22-1420 guardianship files.

**Dufferin County:** RG 22-346 index; RG 22-347 non-contentious business books; RG 22-348 grant book; RG 22-349 guardianship register; RG 22-350 guardianship files; RG 22-352 order book; RG 22-362 estate files; RG 22-407 registers; RG 22-1575 action and matter files.

**Elgin County:** RG 22-322 estate files; RG 22-401 registers.

**Essex County:** RG 22-310 registers; RG 22-311 estate files; RG 22-312 filings; RG 22-792 contentious estate files; RG 22-1848 infant custody applications; RG 22-1870 order book.

**Frontenac County:** RG 22-156 registers; RG 22-157 indexes; RG 22-158 non-contentious business books; RG 22-159 estate files; RG 22-160 filings; RG 22-161 guardianship registers; RG 22-162 process book; RG 22-506 infant custody applications; RG 22-1977 administration bond books.

**Grey County:** RG 22-252 registers; RG 22-253 non-contentious business books; RG 22-254 guardianship book; RG 22-255 minutes; RG 22-356 estate files.

**Haldimand County:** RG 22-256 registers; RG 22-257 indexes; RG 22-258 non-contentious business books; RG 22-259 grant books; RG 22-260 estate files; RG 22-261 filing; RG 22-262 order book; RG 22-2124 court docket and order books; RG 22-2145 action and matter files; RG 22-2176 administration bond books; RG 22-2040 caveat book; RG 22-2041 infant custody applications.

**Halton County:** RG 22-344 minute and order books; RG 22-380 estate files; RG 22-382 grant books; RG 22-383 non-contentious business books; RG 22-2248 administration bond books; RG 22-2249 registers.

**Hastings County:** RG 22-339 registers; RG 22-340 estate files; RG 22-341 filings; RG 22-342 guardianship registers and bond books; RG 22-343 minutes; RG 22-374 non-contentious business books; RG 22-375 index; RG 22-376 grant book; RG 22-377 guardianship files; RG 22-2308 process book; RG 22-2359 Supreme Court estate files; RG 22-2360 caveat book; RG 22-2367 administration files; RG 22-2369 contentious estate files; RG 22-2688 contentious book.

**Huron County:** RG 22-296 registers; RG 22-297 non-contentious business books; RG 22-298 estate files; RG 22-299 guardianship book and register; RG 22-300 caveat book; RG 22-301 procedure book; RG 22-2476 administration bond books; RG 22-2477 action and matter files.

**Kenora District:** RG 22-351 index; RG 22-363 estate files.

**Kent County:** RG 22-395 indexes; RG 22-396 registers; RG 22-397 estate files; RG 22-2678 contentious estate files; RG 22-2687 caveat book; RG 22-2689 executors book; RG 22-2691 guardianship book; RG 22-2693 guardianship register; RG 22-2694 order book.

**Lambton County:** RG 22-269 registers; RG 22-270 indexes; RG 22-271 non-contentious business and grant books; RG 22-272 grant books; RG 22-273 estate files; RG 22-274 filings; RG 22-275 guardianship registers; RG 22-276 guardianship files; RG 22-277 process books; RG 22-278 order and judgment book; RG 22-529 action and matter files; RG 22-2771 succession duty affidavits; RG 22-2773 administration bond books.

**Lanark County:** RG 22-164 registers; RG 22-165 indexes; RG 22-166 non-contentious business books; RG 22-167 grant books; RG 22-168 estate files; RG 22-169 filings; RG 22-170 guardianship books; RG 22-171 caveat book; RG 22-172 process book; RG 22-173 order and minute books; RG 22-174 Lanark and Renfrew United Counties fee books; RG 22-2877 administration bond books; RG 22-2878 guardianship bond book; RG 22-2879 registrar's docket books; RG 22-2880 succession duty affidavits.

**Leeds and Grenville United Counties:** RG 22-175 indexes; RG 22-176 registers; RG 22-177 grant books; RG 22-178 non-contentious business books; RG 22-179 estate files; RG 22-180 filings; RG 22-181 guardianship files; RG 22-182 minutes; RG 22-2913 court docket books; RG 22-2971 process book; RG 22-2975 action and matter files; RG 22-2976 limited partnership records; RG 22-2977 caveat book.

**Lennox and Addington County:** RG 22-249 registers; RG 22-250 non-contentious business books; RG 22-251 guardianship book; RG 22-355 estate files; RG 22-539 action and matter files; RG 22-3076 administration bond books.

**Lincoln County:** RG 22-234 registers; RG 22-235 estate files; RG 22-236 filings; RG 22-237 index; RG 22-238 non-contentious business books; RG 22-239 guardianship registers; RG 22-240 guardianship files; RG 22-241 minutes; RG 22-3166 action files; RG 22-3168 succession duty affidavits.

**Manitoulin District:** RG 22-335 indexes; RG 22-336 grant book; RG 22-337 guardianship book; RG 22-338 process book; RG 22-361 estate files; RG 22-3274 registers.

**Middlesex County:** RG 22-320 registers; RG 22-321 estate files; RG 22-3361 contentious estate files; RG 22-3362 administration bond books; RG 22-3363 grant books; RG 22-3365 judgment and order books; RG 22-3367 succession duty affidavits.

**Muskoka District:** RG 22-365 estate files; RG 22-394 grant book; RG 22-3465 infant custody applications; RG 22-3473 succession duty affidavits; RG 22-3478 non-contentious business book.

**Nipissing District:** RG 22-366 estate files; RG 22-667 action and matter files; RG 22-3561 registers.

**Norfolk County:** RG 22-226 registers; RG 22-227 non-contentious business and grant books and general index; RG 22-228 estate files; RG 22-229 filings; RG 22-230 guardianship book and index; RG 22-231 guardianship files; RG 22-232 minutes; RG 22-233 fee books; RG 22-550 action and matter files; RG 22-3657 order and judgment books; RG 22-3660 estate audit and civil assize rough note books; RG 22-3694 fee book.

**Northumberland and Durham United Counties:** RG 22-187 registers; RG 22-188 indexes; RG 22-189 non-contentious business books; RG 22-190 grant books; RG 22-191 estate files; RG 22-192 filings; RG 22-193 guardianship books; RG 22-3753 administration and guardianship bond books; RG 22-3759 succession duty affidavits; RG 22-3767 order books.

**Ontario County:** RG 22-263 non-contentious business books; RG 22-264 estate files; RG 22-265 filings; RG 22-371 guardianship files; RG 22-782 registers; RG 22-783 registrar's fee book; RG 22-785 grant books; RG 22-786 guardianship book; RG 22-3874 passing of accounts records; RG 22-3875 contentious estate files; RG 22-3876 succession duty affidavits.

**Oxford County:** RG 22-217 registers; RG 22-218 indexes; RG 22-219 grant books; RG 22-220 non-contentious business and grant books; RG 22-221 estate files; RG 22-222 guardianship register; RG 22-223 guardianship files; RG 22-510 action and matter files; RG 22-3982 administration bond books.

**Parry Sound District:** RG 22-399 estate files; RG 22-4059 caveat books; RG 22-4062 non-contentious business books; RG 22-4063 process book; RG 22-4070 registers.

**Peel County:** RG 22-328 registers; RG 22-329 non-contentious business books; RG 22-330 grant books; RG 22-359 estate files; RG 22-509 action and matter files; RG 22-4110 judgments and orders and submissions microfilm; RG 22-4138 guardianship book; RG 22-4139 guardianship files; RG 22-4140 caveat book; RG

22-4141 caveat files; RG 22-4142 procedure book; RG 22-4143 docket books; RG 22-4144 minute books; RG 22-4146 passing of accounts order book; RG 22-4147 administration, guardianship, and bond registers; RG 22-4148 process book.

**Perth County:** RG 22-266 registers; RG 22-267 estate files; RG 22-268 filings; RG 22-4275 action and matter files.

**Peterborough County:** RG 22-242 registers; RG 22-243 non-contentious business books; RG 22-244 grant books; RG 22-245 estate files; RG 22-246 filings; RG 22-247 guardianship files; RG 22-248 process, order, and judgment book; RG 22-511 action and matter files; RG 22-4361 passing of accounts order book; RG 22-4362 administration bond book; RG 22-4363 succession duty affidavits.

**Prescott and Russell United Counties:** RG 22-183 registers; RG 22-184 grant books; RG 22-185 non-contentious business books; RG 22-186 guardianship files; RG 22-353 estate files; RG 22-4461 index; RG 22-4474 order book.

**Prince Edward County:** RG 22-345 guardianship files; RG 22-405 registers; RG 22-406 estate files.

**Rainy River District:** RG 22-368 estate files.

**Renfrew County:** RG 22-364 estate files; RG 22-408 registers; RG 22-174 Lanark and Renfrew United Counties fee books; RG 22-4770 action and matter files.

**Simcoe County:** RG 22-315 estate files; RG 22-316 filings; RG 22-400 registers; RG 22-4837 infant custody applications; RG 22-4871 contentious estate files; RG 22-4874 process books;

RG 22-4875 indexes; RG 22-4878 non-contentious business book; RG 22-4879 grant books.

**Stormont, Dundas, and Glengarry United Counties:** RG 22-194 registers; RG 22-195 indexes; RG 22-196 non-contentious business books; RG 22-197 grant and non-contentious business books; RG 22-198 estate files; RG 22-200 guardianship book and registers; RG 22-4922 local registrar appeal books; RG 22-4971 succession duty affidavits; RG 22-4973 minute book; RG 22-4977 guardianship bond book; RG 22-4978 action and matter files.

**Sudbury District:** RG 22-367 estate files; RG 22-512 registers; RG 22-5048 infant custody applications; RG 22-5068 order books; RG 22-5069 contentious estate files.

**Thunder Bay District:** RG 22-378 registers; RG 22-379 non-contentious business books; RG 22-398 estate files; RG 22-5286 bond book.

**Timiskaming District:** RG 22-369 estate files; RG 22-5147 guardianship bond book; RG 22-5149 registers.

**Victoria County:** RG 22-279 registers; RG 22-280 non-contentious business book; RG 22-281 grant book; RG 22-282 guardianship files; RG 22-357 estate files; RG 22-5335 infant custody applications; RG 22-5380 contentious estate files; RG 22-5381 administration bond books; RG 22-5382 passing of accounts records.

**Waterloo County:** RG 22-211 registers; RG 22-212 non-contentious business and grant books; RG 22-213 grant books; RG 22-214 estate files; RG 22-215 guardianship book; RG 22-216 process and audit books; RG 22-543 action and matter files; RG 22-5473 guardianship register; RG 22-5474 index; RG 22-5475 order books.

**Welland County:** RG 22-286 registers; RG 22-287 non-contentious business books; RG 22-288 grant books; RG 22-289 estate files; RG 22-290 filings; RG 22-291 guardianship books; RG 22-292 guardianship files; RG 22-293 caveat book; RG 22-294 contentious books; RG 22-295 order book; RG 22-5508 minute book; RG 22-5576 administration bond books.

**Wellington County:** RG 22-317 registers; RG 22-318 estate files; RG 22-319 filings; RG 22-5657 order book; RG 22-5663 non-contentious business and grant books.

**Wentworth County:** RG 22-201 indexes; RG 22-202 non-contentious business books; RG 22-203 grant books; RG 22-204 registers; RG 22-205 estate files; RG 22-206 filings; RG 22-207 guardianship book and registers; RG 22-208 guardianship files; RG 22-209 caveat book; RG 22-210 procedure book; RG 22-5776 administration bond books; RG 22-5777 passing of accounts order book; RG 22-5778 process and audit books; RG 22-5780 contentious estate files.

**York County:** RG 22-302 registers; RG 22-303 indexes; RG 22-304 non-contentious business books; RG 22-305 estate files; RG 22-307 caveat book; RG 22-308 minute book; RG 22-309 process book; RG 22-791 application books.

# APPENDIX B

# Published Indexes to Ontario Estate Records

Many genealogical and historical societies and individual authors continue to create indexes to various estate records. Check with local societies and libraries for the latest additions. Note that the June Gibson indexes listed under most counties are also available on three CDs from GlobalGenealogy.com.

**Addington** (see Lennox and Addington)

**Algoma**

*Index to Algoma Wills 1859–1928.* Sault Ste. Marie, ON: OGS, Sault and District Branch, [1984?].

**Brant**

Gibson, June, Elizabeth Hancocks, and Shannon Hancocks. *Surrogate Court Index of Ontario, Canada, 1859–1900, Volume 20, Brant County.* Milton, ON: Global Heritage Press, 2005.

Trace, Mary Kearns. *Names in Lincoln County Probates 1794–1813.* Calgary: Traces, 1986. (Area covered includes Lincoln, Welland, and parts of Wentworth, Haldimand, and Brant counties.)

**Bruce** (pre-1867, see also Huron)

Gibson, June, Elizabeth Hancocks, and Shannon Hancocks. *Surrogate Court Index of Ontario, Canada, 1859–1900, Volume 26, Bruce County.* Milton, ON: Global Heritage Press, 2005.

**Carleton**

Crowder, Norman K. *Early Ottawa Valley Records.* Ottawa: OGS Ottawa Branch, 1988. (Includes indexes to wills in the abstract indexes to deeds for Huntley, Marlborough, and Torbolton townships.)

Gibson, June, Elizabeth Hancocks, and Shannon Hancocks. *Surrogate Court Index of Ontario, Canada, 1859–1900, Volume 6, Carleton County.* Milton, ON: Global Heritage Press, 2005.

**Cochrane**

*Index to Algoma Wills 1859–1928.* Sault Ste. Marie, ON: OGS, Sault and District Branch, [1984?].

**Dufferin** (pre-1881, see Grey, Simcoe, or Wellington counties)

Gibson, June, Elizabeth Hancocks, and Shannon Hancocks. *Surrogate Court Index of Ontario, Canada, 1859–1900, Volume 18, Dufferin County.* Milton, ON: Global Heritage Press, 2005.

**Dundas** (see Stormont, Dundas, and Glengarry)

**Durham** (see Northumberland and Durham)

**Elgin**

Gibson, June, Elizabeth Hancocks, and Shannon Hancocks. *Surrogate Court Index of Ontario, Canada, 1859–1900, Volume 12, Elgin County.* Milton, ON: Global Heritage Press, 2005.

McCallum, James L. *Index to the General Register, Elgin County Land Registry Office.* St. Thomas, ON: OGS Elgin County Branch, 2002–03 (Volume 1: 1866–73, Volume 2: 1873–79, Volume 3: 1879–89). These indexes are also available online at *www.elginogs.ca/Home/ancestor-indexes/online-publications.*

McCallum, James L. *Wills and Probates in Elgin County, Ontario, Land Registry Office Records.* St. Thomas, ON: OGS Elgin County Branch, 2000.

Peters, Stephen J., and Edward Phelps. *Wills of Elgin County, 1845–1852, Vol 1 and 2.* St. Thomas, ON: Elgin County Public Library, 1983–84.

Yeager, William R. *Wills of the London District 1800–1839: An Abstract and Index Guide to the London District Surrogate Registry Registers — Wills and Testamentary Documents.* Simcoe, ON: Norfolk Historical Society, 1979. (Area covered includes Norfolk, Elgin, Haldimand, Oxford, and Middlesex.)

**Essex**

Gibson, June, Elizabeth Hancocks, and Shannon Hancocks. *Surrogate Court Index of Ontario, Canada, 1859–1900, Volume 3, Kent and Essex Counties.* Milton, ON: Global Heritage Press, 2005.

**Frontenac**

Corupe, Linda. *Index to the Intestate Surrogate Files of Frontenac County, Ont. 1821–1869.* Bolton, ON: Linda Corupe, 1997.

Gibson, June, Elizabeth Hancocks, and Shannon Hancocks. *Surrogate Court Index of Ontario, Canada, 1859–1900, Volume 8, Frontenac County.* Milton, ON: Global Heritage Press, 2005.

*Index to Wills Probated, Frontenac County, Ontario, Canada, 1858–1973: A Transcription of the Original Abstract Index Books.* Kingston, ON: OGS Kingston Branch, 1988.

Wanamaker, Loral, and Mildred Wannamaker. *Abstracts of Surrogate Court Wills: Kingston and Vicinity, 1790–1858*. Kingston, ON: OGS Kingston Branch, 1982.

**Glengarry** (see Stormont, Dundas, and Glengarry)

**Grenville** (see Leeds and Grenville)

**Grey**

Gibson, June, Elizabeth Hancocks, and Shannon Hancocks. *Surrogate Court Index of Ontario, Canada, 1859–1900, Volume 27, Grey County*. Milton, ON: Global Heritage Press, 2005.

**Haldimand**

Gibson, June, Elizabeth Hancocks, and Shannon Hancocks. *Surrogate Court Index of Ontario, Canada, 1859–1900, Volume 10, Haldimand County*. Milton, ON: Global Heritage Press, 2005.

Trace, Mary Kearns. *Names in Lincoln County Probates 1794–1813*. Calgary: Traces, 1986. (Area covered includes Lincoln, Welland, and parts of Wentworth, Haldimand, and Brant counties.)

Yeager, William R. *Wills of the London District 1800–1839: An Abstract and Index Guide to the London District Surrogate Registry Registers — Wills and Testamentary Documents*. Simcoe, ON: Norfolk Historical Society, 1979. (Area covered includes Norfolk, Elgin, Haldimand, Oxford, and Middlesex.)

**Haliburton** (see Victoria)

**Halton**

Gibson, June, Elizabeth Hancocks, and Shannon Hancocks. *Surrogate Court Index of Ontario, Canada, 1859–1900, Volume 23, Halton County*. Milton, ON: Global Heritage Press, 2005.

Knight, Lois. *Name Index for Halton County Surrogate Court Probate Papers.* [Brampton?]: OGS Halton-Peel Branch, [19——].

## Hastings

Gibson, June, Elizabeth Hancocks, and Shannon Hancocks. *Surrogate Court Index of Ontario, Canada, 1859–1900, Volume 2, Hastings and Prince Edward Counties.* Milton, ON: Global Heritage Press, 2005.

## Huron

Gibson, June, Elizabeth Hancocks, and Shannon Hancocks. *Surrogate Court Index of Ontario, Canada, 1859–1900, Volume 25, Huron County.* Milton, ON: Global Heritage Press, 2005.

## Kenora

*Index to Algoma Wills 1859–1928.* Sault Ste. Marie, ON: OGS, Sault and District Branch, [1984?].

## Kent

Gibson, June, Elizabeth Hancocks, and Shannon Hancocks. *Surrogate Court Index of Ontario, Canada, 1859–1900, Volume 3, Kent and Essex Counties.* Milton, ON: Global Heritage Press, 2005.

## Lambton

Gibson, June, Elizabeth Hancocks, and Shannon Hancocks. *Surrogate Court Index of Ontario, Canada, 1859–1900, Volume 15, Lambton County.* Milton, ON: Global Heritage Press, 2005.

## Lanark

Gibson, June, Elizabeth Hancocks, and Shannon Hancocks. *Surrogate Court Index of Ontario, Canada, 1859–1900, Volume 16, Lanark County.* Milton, ON: Global Heritage Press, 2005.

## Leeds and Grenville

Gibson, June, Elizabeth Hancocks, and Shannon Hancocks. *Surrogate Court Index of Ontario, Canada, 1859–1900, Volume 22, Leeds and Grenville County.* Milton, ON: Global Heritage Press, 2005.

## Lennox and Addington

Gibson, June, Elizabeth Hancocks, and Shannon Hancocks. *Surrogate Court Index of Ontario, Canada, 1859–1900, Volume 9, Lennox and Addington County.* Milton, ON: Global Heritage Press, 2005.

## Lincoln

Gibson, June, Elizabeth Hancocks, and Shannon Hancocks. *Surrogate Court Index of Ontario, Canada, 1859–1900, Volume 5, Lincoln and Welland Counties.* Milton, ON: Global Heritage Press, 2005.

Kanen-Smith, Shirley. *General Register from Niagara South Registry Office #59, Welland, Ontario.* St. Catharines, ON: SYCAM Pub., circa 1999–[2001?].

Robbins, Douglas A. *Wills Registered in Lincoln County 1801–1920.* St. Catharines, ON: Douglas A. Robbins, 1992.

Taylor, Corlene Dwyer. *Estate Files of Lincoln County, Ontario, Canada 1794 to 1858 [and] Index to Surrogate Court Register of Lincoln (and Welland) County [1793–1859].* [Beamsville?]: House of Dwyer, 2002.

Trace, Mary Kearns. *Names in Lincoln County Probates 1794–1813.* Calgary: Traces, 1986. (Area covered includes Lincoln, Welland, and parts of Wentworth, Haldimand, and Brant counties.)

## Manitoulin

*Index to Algoma Wills 1859–1928.* Sault Ste. Marie, ON: OGS, Sault and District Branch, [1984?].

## Middlesex

Yeager, William R. *Wills of the London District 1800–1839: An Abstract and Index Guide to the London District Surrogate Registry Registers — Wills and Testamentary Documents.* Simcoe, ON: Norfolk Historical Society, 1979. (Area includes Norfolk, Elgin, Haldimand, Oxford, and Middlesex.)

## Muskoka

No published index found. See neighbouring counties.

## Nipissing

No published index found. See neighbouring counties.

## Norfolk

Calder, Robert W., and Dan Walker. *Wills in the Norfolk Land Registry Office 1799–1900.* Delhi, ON: Norsim Research & Publishing, 1995.

Gibson, June, Elizabeth Hancocks, and Shannon Hancocks. *Surrogate Court Index of Ontario, Canada, 1859–1900, Volume 1, Norfolk County.* Milton, ON: Global Heritage Press, 2005.

Yeager, William R. *Wills of the London District 1800–1839: An Abstract and Index Guide to the London District Surrogate Registry Registers — Wills and Testamentary Documents.* Simcoe, ON: Norfolk Historical Society, 1979. (Area covered includes Norfolk, Elgin, Haldimand, Oxford, and Middlesex.)

## Northumberland and Durham

Gibson, June, Elizabeth Hancocks, and Shannon Hancocks. *Surrogate Court Index of Ontario, Canada, 1859–1900, Volume 4, Northumberland and Durham Counties.* Milton, ON: Global Heritage Press, 2005.

## Ontario

Gibson, June, Elizabeth Hancocks, and Shannon Hancocks. *Surrogate Court Index of Ontario, Canada, 1859–1900, Volume 11, Ontario County*. Milton, ON: Global Heritage Press, 2005.

## Oxford

Adam, Pat. *Index to Guardianship Papers, Surrogate Court, Oxford County 1859–1868*. [Woodstock, ON]: OGS Oxford Branch, [1980?].

Bonk, Darryl. *Wills of Oxford County 1805–1870*. [Woodstock, ON]: OGS Oxford Branch, 1980.

*Index to Oxford County Wills, Registers 1 to 11, 1853 to 1902*, and *Index to Oxford County Wills, 1901 to 1930* (available online at *www.ogs.on.ca/oxford/OnLinePubsOx.html*).

*Oxford County Surrogate Court Estate Files Index 1901–1930*. [Woodstock, ON]: OGS Oxford County Branch, 1999.

Yeager, William R. *Wills of the London District 1800–1839: An Abstract and Index Guide to the London District Surrogate Registry Registers — Wills and Testamentary Documents*. Simcoe, ON: Norfolk Historical Society, 1979. (Area covered includes Norfolk, Elgin, Haldimand, Oxford, and Middlesex.)

## Parry Sound

No published index found. See neighbouring counties.

## Peel

Gibson, June, Elizabeth Hancocks, and Shannon Hancocks. *Surrogate Court Index of Ontario, Canada, 1859–1900, Volume 19, Peel County*. Milton, ON: Global Heritage Press, 2005.

Gilchrist, J. Brian. *Estate Records of Peel County, Ontario, 1813–1867: An Alphabetical Index to the Wills, Administrations and Guardianships Found in the Records of the Probate Court, the Surrogate Court and the Land Registry Office*. Toronto: printed by the author, 2000.

## Perth

Riedstra, Lutzen. *Index to Perth County Wills 1853–1873.* Stratford: OGS Perth County Branch, 1984.

## Peterborough

Gibson, June, Elizabeth Hancocks, and Shannon Hancocks. *Surrogate Court Index of Ontario, Canada, 1859–1900, Volume 17, Peterborough County.* Milton, ON: Global Heritage Press, 2005.

Hansen, Tina. *Peterborough Wills 1868–1880.* Peterborough, ON: KARA, 1999.

## Prescott and Russell

Gibson, June, Elizabeth Hancocks, and Shannon Hancocks. *Surrogate Court Index of Ontario, Canada, 1859–1900, Volume 14, Prescott and Russell Counties.* Milton, ON: Global Heritage Press, 2005.

## Prince Edward

Gibson, June, Elizabeth Hancocks, and Shannon Hancocks. *Surrogate Court Index of Ontario, Canada, 1859–1900, Volume 2, Hastings and Prince Edward Counties.* Milton, ON: Global Heritage Press, 2005.

## Rainy River

*Index to Algoma Wills 1859–1928.* Sault Ste. Marie, ON: OGS, Sault and District Branch, [1984?].

## Renfrew

Wohler, Patrick. *Index of Probated Wills for Renfrew County 1878–1969.* [Arnprior, ON]: Arnprior & McNab/Braeside Archives, 2009 (CD).

**Russell** (see Prescott and Russell)

## Simcoe

Purvis, Jack, and Helen Wanless. *Index to Probate and Surrogate Court Records, Simcoe County 1828–1929.* Barrie, ON: OGS Simcoe County Branch, 1988. (Reissued on CD in 2007.)

## Stormont, Dundas, and Glengarry

Gibson, June, Elizabeth Hancocks, and Shannon Hancocks. *Surrogate Court Index of Ontario, Canada, 1859–1900, Volume 7, Stormont, Dundas and Glengarry Counties.* Milton, ON: Global Heritage Press, 2005.

## Sudbury

*Sudbury Land Registry Office Registered Wills.* Sudbury, ON: OGS Sudbury District Branch, 2004.

*Index to Algoma Wills 1859–1928.* Sault Ste. Marie, ON: OGS, Sault and District Branch, [1984?].

## Temiskaming

*Index to Algoma Wills 1859–1928.* Sault Ste. Marie, ON: OGS, Sault and District Branch, [1984?].

## Thunder Bay

*Index to Algoma Wills 1859–1928.* Sault Ste. Marie, ON: OGS, Sault and District Branch, [1984?].

**Victoria** (includes Haliburton)

Gibson, June, Elizabeth Hancocks, and Shannon Hancocks. *Surrogate Court Index of Ontario, Canada, 1859–1900, Volume 21, Victoria County.* Milton, ON: Global Heritage Press, 2005.

## Waterloo

Gibson, June, Elizabeth Hancocks, and Shannon Hancocks. *Surrogate Court Index of Ontario, Canada, 1859–1900, Volume 13, Waterloo County.* Milton, ON: Global Heritage Press, 2005.

Waterloo County Entries to 1858 (available online at *www.waterlooOGS.ca/Wills/Willsto1858.PDF.*)

McKnight, David R. *Waterloo Wills: A Genealogical Index of Wills and Estate Documents [in] 19th Century Land Registry Office Records, County of Waterloo, 2nd revised edition.* Kitchener, ON: OGS Waterloo-Wellington Branch, 1997. (Electronic version by Shawn D. McKnight, published circa 2005.)

## Welland

Gibson, June, Elizabeth Hancocks, and Shannon Hancocks. *Surrogate Court Index of Ontario, Canada, 1859–1900, Volume 5, Lincoln and Welland Counties.* Milton, ON: Global Heritage Press, 2005.

Kanen-Smith, Shirley. *General Register from Niagara South Registry Office #59, Welland, Ontario.* St. Catharines, ON: SYCAM Pub., circa 1999–[2001?].

Taylor, Corlene Dwyer. *Estate Files of Lincoln County, Ontario, Canada 1794 to 1858 [and] Index to Surrogate Court Register of Lincoln (and Welland) County [1793–1859].* [Beamsville]: House of Dwyer, 2002.

Trace, Mary Kearns. *Names in Lincoln County Probates 1794–1813.* Calgary: Traces, 1986. (Area covered includes Lincoln, Welland, and parts of Wentworth, Haldimand, and Brant counties.)

*Wills and Probate from the Land Registry Copy Books, Welland County 1793–1875.* St. Catharines, ON: OGS Niagara Peninsula Branch, 1993.

## Wellington

Gibson, June, Elizabeth Hancocks, and Shannon Hancocks. *Surrogate Court Index of Ontario, Canada, 1859–1900, Volume 24, Wellington County*. Milton, ON: Global Heritage Press, 2005.

## Wentworth

Trace, Mary Kearns. *Names in Lincoln County Probates 1794–1813*. Calgary: Traces, 1986. (Area covered includes Lincoln, Welland, and parts of Wentworth, Haldimand, and Brant counties.)

*Wills from the East Flamborough Registry Abstract Index Books, Books 1–5, 1796–1956*. Waterdown, ON: Waterdown-East Flamborough Heritage Society, 2000.

*Wills from the West Flamborough Registry Abstract Index Books, Books 1–5, 1796–1969*. Waterdown, ON: Waterdown-East Flamborough Heritage Society, 2000.

## York

Gilchrist, J. Brian. *Estate records of the City of Toronto and the County of York, 1800–1864: being an alphabetical index to wills, administrations and guardianships found in the records of the York County Surrogate Court*. (Anticipated publication date, 2013.)

# INDEX

Equity court (*see* Chancery, Court of)

Essex County Surrogate Court, 83, 108

Estate files, 72–75

  analysis of, 23–36, 60–61, 74, 80–81

  Court of Probate, 58–62

  less than 40 years old, 79

  photo of, 58

  surrogate courts, 79–81

Estate records, ancillary probate, 99

  determining which court to search, 17–18

  in manuscript collections, 104–05

  in newspapers, 98–101

  in other jurisdictions, 97–99

  jargon, 22

  laws regarding, 20–21

  locations of, 18–20

  value for genealogical research, 11–13

Everitt, Capt. P., 52

Executors, definition of, 22

Falkner, William, 51

Family History Library (*see* FamilySearch.org)

FamilySearch.org, address, 18

  Court of Probate microfilms, 61–63

  land records on microfilm, 90

  Luneburg District Prerogative Court microfilm, 51

  surrogate courts microfilms, 71, 75–76, 81

Faulkner, William, 52–53

Field(s), Daniel, 50

Fitzgibbon, Charles, 63

Fraser, James, 47–50

  Thos, 53

French civil law, 43–44, 67, 90

Frontenac County Surrogate Court, 77, 83, 108

Gagnier, Jacques, 47

Gay, Edward, 54

Genié, François, 48

  Honoré, 48

Girardin, Jean François, 50

Godfrey, Gabriel, 48

Gore District, 69

Gouget, Joseph, 48

Goyeaux, Caterine, 48

  Lois, 48

  Nicolas, 48

Granger, Jacques, 47

Grant books (*see* Registers of grants)

Gray, Edward William, 48

  James, 52

Greverat, Garret, 48

Grey County Surrogate Court, 109

Groesbeck, William, 48

Guardianship records (*see also* Tuteurs), 45, 59, 68, 87–88, 99, 107–15

Haldimand County Surrogate Court, 109

Halton County Surrogate Court, 109

Hamilton, Robert, 55

Hamilton and Cartwright, merchants, 39

Hands, William, 47, 49

Harffy, Doctor, 49

Harper, Sally, 93

Harsen, Jacob, 48

Hastings County Surrogate Court, 77, 83, 109

Heir and Devisee Commissions, 101–04

# Index

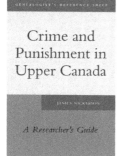

## CRIME AND PUNISHMENT IN UPPER CANADA
### A Researcher's Guide
Janice Nickerson
978-1554887705 $19.99
This reference provides genealogists and social historians with context and tools to locate sources on criminal activity and its consequences for the Upper Canada period (1791–1841) of Ontario's history. An entertaining, educational read, it features chapters with detailed inventories of available records in federal, provincial, and local repositories; published and online transcripts and indices; and suggestions for additional reading.

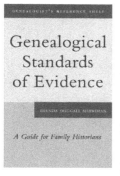

## GENEALOGICAL STANDARDS OF EVIDENCE
### A Guide for Family Historians
Brenda Dougall Merriman
978-1554884513 $19.99
This guide takes readers through the genealogical process of research and identification, along the way examining how the genealogical community has developed standards of evidence and documentation, what the standards are, and how they can be applied. A perfect supplement to courses, workshops, and seminars, this book provides an in-depth reference perfect for compiling and checking notes.

## CONSERVING, PRESERVING, AND RESTORING YOUR HERITAGE
### A Professional's Advice
Kennis Kim
978-1554884629 $19.99

Our family history may be held in documents, photographs, books, clothing, or textiles; sometimes complete collections of items such as coins, trading cards, or stamps. As custodians of pieces of our history, we are faced with how to maintain these items. Here's all you need to determine what you can do yourself to preserve your precious things for future generations.

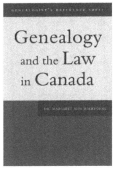

## GENEALOGY AND THE LAW IN CANADA
Dr. Margaret Ann Wilkinson
978-1554884520 $19.99

The development of digital records and broad access to the web has revolutionized the ways in which genealogists approach their investigations — and has made it much easier to locate relevant information. The law, on the other hand, remains very connected to particular geographic locations. This book discusses the relevant laws — access to information, protection of personal data, and copyright — applicable to those working within Canada with materials that are located in Canada.

## PUBLISH YOUR FAMILY HISTORY
### Preserving Your Heritage in a Book
Susan Yates and Greg Ioannou
978-1554887279 $19.99

Many people want to write a family history, but few ever take on the job of publishing one. *Publish Your Family History* will tell you all the fundamentals of book production, together with the important details that distinguish a home-published book from a homemade one.

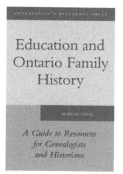

## EDUCATION AND ONTARIO FAMILY HISTORY
### A Guide to Resources for Genealogists and Historians
Marian Press
978-1554887477 $19.99

This book outlines the resources available for education from about 1785 to the early twentieth century. Many historical resources are currently being digitized, and Ontario and education are no exception. These electronic repositories are examined here, along with traditional paper and archival sources.

## A CALL TO THE COLOURS
### Tracing Your Canadian Military Ancestors
Ken Cox
978-1554888641 $19.99

Our ancestors were required to perform military service, often as militia. The discovery that an ancestor served during one of the major conflicts in our history is exciting. *A Call to the Colours* provides the archival, library, and computer resources that can be employed to explore your family's military history.

## TIME TRAVELLER'S HANDBOOK
### A Guide to the Past
Althea Douglas
978-1554887842 $19.99

This book considers documents and how to look at papers and artifacts that have survived over the years, as well as those family legends and mythinformation handed down by word of mouth, and how to avoid wasting time wading through this sort of information.

VISIT US AT
*Dundurn.com*
*Definingcanada.ca*
*@dundurnpress*
*Facebook.com/dundurnpress*